Breaks in Europe

ROUGH GUIDES

NEW YORK • LONDON • DELHI

www.roughguides.com

Credits

Written in association with Dove ProAge

Editor (Rough Guides): Jules Brown
Text: Helena Smith, based on information contained in the Rough Guide to Europe
Project Manager: Carolyn Smith
Cover design: Philippa Hopkins and Diana Jarvis
Design and layout: Diana Jarvis
Proofreader: Helen Castell
Production: Aimee Hampson
Picture editors: Philippa Hopkins, Emma Traynor & Jj Luck

Publishing information:
Published 2007 by Rough Guides Ltd, 80 Strand, London WC2R 0RL
Printed in Italy by Legoprint S.p.A

Cover image credits:
Front cover Bicycle and tulips Amsterdam, Netherlands, © MARC ROMANELLI/Alamy
Back cover Gondolier awaiting passengers © Diana Jarvis

The **Rough Guide** to

Relaxing Mini Breaks in Europe

Contents

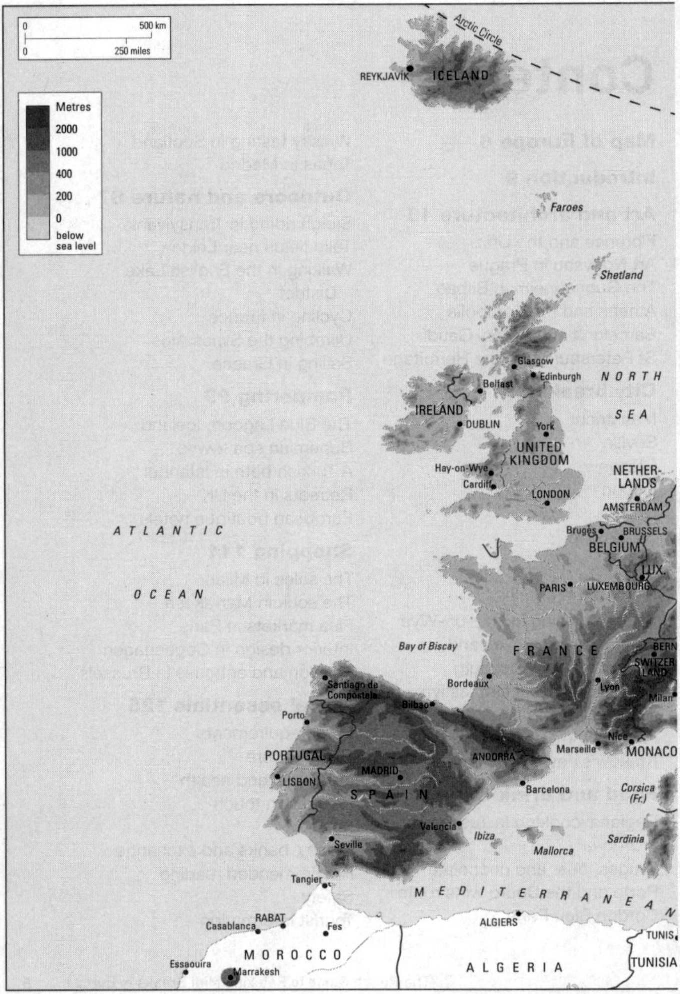
0
500 km
0
250 miles
Metres
2000
1000
400
200
0
below sea level
Arctic Circle
REYKJAVIK
ICELAND
Faroes
Shetland
Glasgow
Edinburgh
NORTH
SEA
Belfast
IRELAND
DUBLIN
York
UNITED KINGDOM
Hay-on-Wye
Cardiff
LONDON
NETHER-LANDS
AMSTERDAM
Bruges
BRUSSELS
BELGIUM
LUX.
LUXEMBOURG
PARIS
ATLANTIC
OCEAN
Bay of Biscay
FRANCE
BERN
SWITZERLAND
Lyon
Milan
Bordeaux
Santiago de Compostela
Bilbao
Porto
PORTUGAL
ANDORRA
Nice
Marseille
MONACO
MADRID
LISBON
SPAIN
Barcelona
Corsica (Fr.)
Valencia
Ibiza
Sardinia
Seville
Mallorca
Tangier
MEDITERRANEAN
RABAT
Casablanca
Fes
ALGIERS
TUNIS
MOROCCO
ALGERIA
TUNISIA
Essaouira
Marrakesh

NORWAY
SWEDEN
FINLAND
RUSSIA
OSLO
STOCKHOLM
HELSINKI
St Petersburg
TALLINN
ESTONIA
BALTIC SEA
Gothenburg
RĪGA
LATVIA
MOSCOW
DENMARK
COPENHAGEN
LITHUANIA
KALININGRAD (RUSSIA)
VILNIUS
Hamburg
MINSK
BELARUS
BERLIN
GERMANY
WARSAW
POLAND
Frankfurt
KIEV
Kraków
PRAGUE
CZECH REPUBLIC
UKRAINE
SLOVAKIA
Munich
Salzburg
VIENNA
BRATISLAVA
MOLDOVA
CHIŞINĂU
BUDAPEST
AUSTRIA
HUNGARY
LJUBLJANA
ROMANIA
Venice
SLOVENIA
ZAGREB
CROATIA
GEORGIA
SAN MARINO
BOSNIA-HERZEGOVINA
BELGRADE
BUCHAREST
BLACK SEA
Florence
SARAJEVO
SERBIA & MONTENEGRO
BULGARIA
ITALY
Adriatic Sea
SOFIA
ROME
ALBANIA
MACEDONIA
İstanbul
Naples
TIRANA
Thessaloniki
ANKARA
TURKEY
Corfu
GREECE
Aegean Sea
İzmir
ATHENS
Cyclades
SEA
Sicily
SYRIA
MALTA
Crete
Rhodes
CYPRUS
LEBANON

Introduction

Whether you need help recovering from Christmas, have made a New Year's resolution to learn something new, or simply want some fresh ideas for fun travel, the **Rough Guide to Relaxing Mini Breaks in Europe** is designed to help. We've covered every corner of the continent in the search for stress-free leisure, and think that we've turned up something for everyone, from Lisbon to Stockholm, Dublin to Prague. Admittedly, we're a little eccentric when it comes to defining what is and what isn't in Europe – St Petersburg, arguably, Morocco and Turkey, not strictly speaking – but every destination in the guide is easily accessible on a short break, and offers the prospect of a real retreat from the daily grind. With budget airlines spreading their tentacles ever wider across Europe, flying is often going to be the quickest and most convenient option, but in the spirit of reducing our carbon footprint we've also shown where taking the train is just as good, or even better. From the new Eurostar terminal at London St Pancras you can be in Brussels or Paris in just a couple of hours, with onward connections across Europe widely available – and why hang about at airports when your relaxing break can start the minute you board the train?

Of course, one person's idea of relaxation is another's vision of hard work so we've tried to give as wide a range of options as we can. Hitting the January sales in Milan or cooking up a storm at the Cordon Bleu cookery school in Paris might not be your cup of tea – indeed, perspiration may already be forming on your brow at the very thought – so what about taking a Turkish bath in İstanbul, or enjoying a lazy weekend's book-browsing in Hay-on-Wye? And even if you think you know all there is to know about a destination – whether a favoured city or resort – we hope we can show you a different way of looking at things.

We've arranged the guide thematically, so you can hone in easily on your interests – or explore new ones. In **art and architecture** we've highlighted some quintessential European attractions, from touring Antoni Gaudí's other-worldly buildings in Barcelona to a stroll around Italy's finest gallery, the Uffizi in Florence. With the proliferation in European budget airlines, **city breaks** go from strength to strength but in our "weekend-away" section we've tried to point you towards places that are a little more off the radar – Seville, Nice, Maastricht and even Glasgow are all ideal for a quick jaunt at any time of year and just might surprise you. There are plenty of other cities covered in this book, too, each of which could keep visitors busy for weeks, but our advice is not to try to do too much. Concentrate on one or two museums, or a particular festival or event that engages your interest, or simply wander the streets out of season and take things easy in a café. After all, you're on holiday.

There's an eclectic mix of experiences available in our **culture** section – sign up for a writing course in Ireland, get the lowdown on Berlin's annual film festival, make the Mozart connection in Salzburg or dig out your gladrags for Vienna's celebrated ball season. In **food and drink** it's all about expanding the senses and pursuing new tastes – if you've never given much thought to beer or whisky we've got tours in Belgium and Scotland that might just change your mind, while accounts of Tuscan cooking schools and Madrid's tapas bars offer a close-up insight into some of Europe's finest food.

For some, relaxation comes at the end of a day's gentle activity, so in **outdoors and nature** we look at a selection of easygoing outdoor trips, from hiking in the English Lake District to sleigh-riding in Transylvania. You'll find full details of tour operators who can make all the arrangements – all you have to do is pack. If your goal instead is a bit of honest-to-goodness **pampering**, then you could opt for a yoga break, spa trip or even a retreat in the British countryside – this guide has all three experiences covered, along with a rundown of some of Europe's finest boutique hotels, where style holds sway. Finally, it goes without saying that retail therapy is the ultimate form of relaxation for many, so in the **shopping** section we tell you how to negotiate the souk in Marrakesh, scour the flea markets in Paris or trawl the annual Antiques Fair in Brussels.

In every section of the guide we've suggested **useful contacts** to help you plan your holiday – from local tourist office websites to specialist tour operators. **Feature boxes** highlight different aspects of each destination, whether it's a list of recommended cafés, details of local festivals or some ideas for day-trips. There's also a **Travel essentials** section at the back of the guide, for pointers on booking transport, accessing money abroad, buying insurance and other useful information.

It's generally true that the more planning you do in advance the smoother your trip is likely to be – to which end, you'll find much more information about every destination covered in the book in our **Rough Guide to Europe** or in one of our dedicated guides to individual European countries and regions (all available to buy from Ⓦwww.roughguides.com). So, read on – and start packing.

Art and architecture

Art and architecture

Florence and the Uffizi
Art Nouveau in Prague
The Guggenheim in Bilbao
Athens and the Acropolis
Barcelona and Antoni Gaudí
St Petersburg and the Hermitage

Florence and the Uffizi

Ever since the nineteenth-century revival of interest in Renaissance art, **Florence** has been a shrine to the cult of the beautiful. It is a city of incomparable indoor pleasures, its chapels, galleries and museums embodying the complex, exhilarating and often elusive spirit of the Renaissance more fully than any other place in Italy. And in the **Galleria degli Uffizi** (Ⓦ www.virtualuffizi.com), Florence has simply the greatest picture gallery in the country, displaying some of the most famous works in Western art.

You can book tickets in advance through the gallery and, especially in summer, you'd be wise to do so as you don't want to waste time queuing. Also note that the collection of masterpieces is vast – almost impossible to take in on a single visit – so plan to return a second time if you can. Most visitors make a beeline for Botticelli: in the *Birth of Venus*, the goddess poses coyly on her scallop shell, while the equally stunning *Primavera* is a joyous allegory of spring. Works from the early Renaissance include

Florence's other galleries

The **Bargello** (Ⓦ www.polomuseale.firenze.it/english/musei/bargello), just north of the Uffizi, focuses the first part of its collection on Michelangelo, while upstairs is Donatello's sexually ambiguous bronze *David*, the first freestanding nude figure since classical times, cast in the early 1430s. The famous **Accademia** (Ⓦ www.weekendafirenze.com/museidet/accademia_e.htm), Europe's first school of drawing, is usually swamped by people who have come to view Michelangelo's *David* (1504) – carved from a single block of marble, when the artist was just 29, it's an incomparable show of technical bravura. The church of Santa Maria del Carmine is an essential visit for the superbly restored frescoes by Masaccio in its **Cappella Brancacci**, while the massive bulk of the fifteenth-century Palazzo Pitti contains no fewer than six separate museums, of which the best is the **Galleria Palatina** (Ⓦ www.polomuseale.firenze.it/english/musei/palatina), which includes a number of Titian's most trenchant portraits.

three gleaming altarpieces of the *Madonna Enthroned* by Cimabue, Duccio and Giotto, though it's Filippo Lippi's *Madonna and Child with Two Angels* that's one of the best-known Renaissance images of the Madonna, with its chubby infant, mischievous cherubs and demure Madonna. While the Uffizi doesn't own a finished painting that's entirely by Leonardo da Vinci, there's a celebrated *Annunciation* that's mainly by him, as well as the beautiful angel in profile that he painted, as a very young apprentice, in Verrocchio's *Baptism*. Other artists represented in the gallery include Caravaggio, Raphael, Rubens, Rembrandt, Dürer and Goya.

Alitalia and other European airlines fly to Florence's airport, though budget airlines, like easyJet, tend to use nearby Pisa instead (80km away), from where there's a direct train to Florence central station. The official **tourist office website** (®www.firenzeturismo.it) is a good place to start planning your trip. There's more detailed information about the Uffizi and Florence's other galleries there, as well as fully searchable lists of accommodation, restaurants and more. The sheer amount of major artworks in the city can soon overwhelm you on a short trip, but Florence has plenty of other diversions: have a wander across the picturesque thirteenth-century **Ponte Vecchio**, loaded with jewellers' shops overhanging the water, which leads from the city centre across the river to the district of Oltrarno, or head for an atmospheric *vinaio*, a wine cellar that serves delicious Tuscan wines and snacks. As for **festivals**, in May there's the *Maggio Musicale* (®www.maggiofiorentino.com), while the *Festa di San Giovanni* on June 24, Florence's saint's day, sees a massive fireworks display. Throughout the summer free concerts and events take place around the city.

Art Nouveau in Prague

Few other cities in Europe look so good as **Prague**. Moreover, provided you're wrapped up warmly, this is a terrific city to visit in the winter months – the crowds won't overwhelm you, the hearty cuisine is suited

Art Nouveau, Prague

Prague's café society

The choice of Prague cafés is pretty varied – from Art Nouveau beauties and swish espresso bars to simple sugar and caffeine joints. Those redolent of the city's glory days include:

Café Imperial Na poříčí 15, Staré Město. An endearingly shabby yet grand Habsburg-era coffee-house, which has retained its original decor.

Café Louvre Národní 20, Nové Město. Restored café with high ceilings, long mirrors, aproned waiters whisking around, the daily papers to read and a billiard hall.

Café Monmartre Retezová 7, Staré Město. A wonderful remnant of the jazz age in Prague – this café was a famous cabaret venue, and has since slipped into atmospheric obscurity.

Obecní dum Nám. Republiky 5, Nové Město. Glorious Art Nouveau decor, impeccable service and a good cake trolley.

to lower temperatures, and nowhere looks prettier sprinkled with snow. easyJet, bmibaby, Jet2.com and other airlines fly here regularly; consult the Prague Information Service (ⓦwww.pis.cz) for help with accommodation and other services.

The city's Art Nouveau treasures can be explored on an informative **Art Nouveau walking tour** run by Prague Sightseeing Tours (ⓦwww.guide-prague.cz). The Czech Art Nouveau or "Secession" movement flowered (quite literally, as it took much inspiration from plant forms) at the beginning of the twentieth century and died with the onset of World War One. Under the communists, Prague's wonderful Art Nouveau legacy began to decay, but many buildings survived and have been restored to their former glory. The movement's characteristics were organic asymmetry, and a celebratory, richly inventive emphasis on the facade – an example is the U Nováku department store, adorned with swirling metalwork, shining mosaics, ornate images of stately peacocks and an elegant stained-glass door.

The most famous Czech practitioner of Art Nouveau was graphic artist and designer Alfons Mucha, who was made famous by the exquisite elongated images of Sarah Bernhardt he drew for her promotional posters;

the **Mucha Museum** (Ⓦwww.mucha.cz) explores his life and work, while you can see more of Mucha's labour at the **Obecní dum** (Ⓦwww.obecnidum.cz), or Municipal House, decorated inside and out with the help of almost every artist connected with Czech Art Nouveau. Guided tours are available of the dramatic interior, covered with mosaics and pendulous chandeliers, or you can have a meal in the French restaurant to the right of the entrance or a coffee in the equally dazzling café.

Other Art Nouveau gems in the city include the sadly decayed main **train station**, with its intriguing stone friezes; the bold **Topic Building** on Národní Třída; and the very splendid **Grand Hotel Evropa** on Wenceslas Square, which retains some original interior fittings.

The Guggenheim in Bilbao

Although traditionally an industrial city, **Bilbao** – biggest city in the Spanish Basque region – has completely reinvented itself over the last decade or so and is now a priority European destination. And no surprise: a state-of-the-art metro (designed by Norman Foster) links the city's widespread attractions, foremost of which is the breathtaking **Guggenheim Museum** (Ⓦwww.guggenheim-bilbao.es) by Frank O. Gehry – ten years old in 2007 and described by architect Philip Johnson as "the greatest building of our time".

Within the sensual, billowing titanium curves are extensive galleries housing the unparalleled permanent collection of twentieth-century art, which includes works by Kandinsky, Klee, Mondrian, Picasso, Chagall, Warhol and others. Temporary exhibitions and individual artists' collections are displayed in the huge sculpted spaces, including Jeff Koons's twelve-foot *Puppy*, a monument to sentimentality, and Louise Bourgeois' elegant but sinister spider sculpture *Maman*. Free guided tours take off daily around the museum, while English-language audio-guides are included in the admission price.

The Guggenheim is at the heart of a redevelopment project that has transformed downtown Bilbao, and it is attracting a growing number of weekenders and art-lovers. easyJet flies here from Stansted, while Ryanair serves Santander, from where there's a connecting bus to Bilbao (1hr 30min). There's plenty more **information** on what to see and do on Ⓦwww.bilbao.net. In particular, the city is a great culinary centre – one of the pre-eminent destinations in Spain for **eating and drinking**. It's particularly celebrated for its *pintxos* (Basque tapas), which you eat moving from bar to bar in the Casco Viejo (old town): the area known as the *siete calles* (seven streets) has numerous options, including the historic Moorish-style *Café Iruña* (c/Jardines de Albia 5) and the excellent *Café Bar Bilbao* (Plaza Nueva 6).

Athens and the Acropolis

Athens has been inhabited continuously for over 7000 years – its Acropolis, protected by a ring of mountains and commanding views of all seagoing approaches, was a natural choice for prehistoric settlement. Its later development as a city-state and artistic centre reached its zenith in the fifth century BC with a flourish of art, architecture, literature and philosophy that has pervaded Western culture ever since.

Most major European airlines have routes to Athens, as does easyJet. Once there, the ancient sites are undoubtedly the city's star attractions, but the pretty cafés, landscaped stair-streets and bustling markets all have their own appeal too. The best time for a visit is spring or autumn, when the crowds have thinned and the temperatures aren't too high. Useful **websites** include those of the Greek National Tourist Organisation (Ⓦwww.gnto.gr); the English-language weekly *Athens News* (Ⓦwww.athensnews.gr); and the government's Ministry of Culture site (Ⓦwww.culture.gr), which has lots of information on the various ruins and museums.

However long you plan to spend in Athens, it simply isn't enough to do the mighty **Acropolis** justice. A rugged limestone outcrop, watered by springs and rising abruptly from the plain of Attica, it was one of the

The Acropolis, Athens

Dining out, the Greek way

Out and about in Athens, you're going to be tempted by the large array of Greek **snacks** available. *Tyrópites* and *spanakópites* (cheese and spinach pies respectively) are on sale everywhere, as are *souvlákia* (small kebabs) and *yíros* (doner kebab), served in *píta* bread with garnish. In choosing a **taverna**, the best strategy is to go where the locals go. Typical dishes to try include *mous-sakás* (aubergine and meat pie), *yígandes* (white haricot beans in red sauce), *tzatzíki* (yoghurt, garlic and cucumber dip), *melit-zanosaláta* (aubergine dip), *khtapódhi* (octopus), and *kalamarákia* (fried baby squid). Note that people eat late: 2.30–4pm for lunch & 9–11.30pm for dinner.

earliest settlements in Greece, and by Mycenaean times sported a fortified palace and temples where the cult of Athena was introduced. During the ninth century BC, it became the heart of the first Greek city-state and, in the wake of Athenian military supremacy and a peace treaty with the Persians in 449 BC, Pericles had the complex reconstructed under the direction of architect and sculptor Pheidias, producing most of the monuments visible today.

Having survived more or less intact for over two millennia, the Acropolis finally fell victim to the vagaries of war. In 1687 besieging Venetians ignited a Turkish gunpowder magazine in the **Parthenon**, blasting off the roof, and in 1801 Lord Elgin removed the frieze (the "Elgin Marbles"), which he later sold to the British Museum. Built on the site of earlier temples, the Parthenon was intended as a new sanctuary for Athena and a house for her cult image, a colossal wooden statue decked in ivory and gold plate that was designed by Pheidias and considered one of the Seven Wonders of the Ancient World; the sculpture was lost in ancient times, but its characteristics are known through later copies.

To the north of the Parthenon stands the **Erechtheion**, the last of the great works of Pericles. Here, in symbolic reconciliation, Athena and the city's previous patron Poseidon-Erechtheus were both worshipped. On the south side, in the Porch of the Caryatids, the Ionic line is transformed into six maidens (caryatids) holding the entablature on their heads.

Placed discreetly on a level below that of the main monuments, the **Acropolis Museum** contains nearly all the portable objects removed from the Acropolis since 1834. The second-century Roman **Odeion of Herodes Atticus**, restored for performances of music and classical drama, dominates the southern slope of the Acropolis hill. The main interest hereabouts lies in earlier Greek sites to the east, pre-eminent among them the **Theatre of Dionysos**. Masterpieces of Aeschylus, Sophocles, Euripides and Aristophanes were first performed here, at one of the most evocative locations in the city. The ruins are impressive; the theatre, rebuilt in the fourth century BC, could hold some 17,000 spectators.

Barcelona and Antoni Gaudí

Barcelona, the self-confident and progressive capital of Catalunya, has a sophistication and cultural dynamism way ahead of the rest of Spain. It's a tremendous place to visit, the most prosperous commercial centre in the country, with some great shopping, 5km of beachfront, and a bar and restaurant scene that has few peers – no wonder it features heavily on the city-break market. But there's more to it than just shops and nightlife, since Barcelona has also evolved an individual and eclectic cultural identity, most perfectly and eccentrically expressed in the surreal buildings of *modernista* architect **Antoni Gaudí** (1852–1926).

Without doubt Gaudí's most famous creation is the incomplete **Temple Expiatori de la Sagrada Família** (Ⓦ www.sagradafamilia.org), his church of the "Sacred Family" which was begun as early as 1882. Construction is still ongoing – not scheduled to finish until 2017 – and the interior is a giant building site, but it's fascinating to watch Gaudí's last-known plans being slowly realized. The size alone is startling, with eight spires rising to over 100m. For Gaudí these symbolized the Twelve Apostles; he planned to build four more above the main facade and to add a 170-metre tower topped with a lamb (representing Jesus) over the transept, itself to be surrounded by four smaller towers symbolizing the Evangelists. Take the lift, or climb up one of the towers, and you can enjoy a dizzy view down over the whole complex and clamber still further round the walls and into the towers.

In the nearby suburb of Gràcia, **Parc Güell** was Gaudí's most ambitious project after the Sagrada Família. This almost hallucinatory experience,

Gaudí architecture, Barcelona

Eat, drink, shop, modernista style

Barcelona's *modernista* architecture provides a fantastic backdrop for eating, drinking and shopping.

Almirall C/Joaquin Costa 33, El Raval. The city's oldest bar (1860) is a fine example of period decor.
Antiga Casa Figueras Ramblas 83, El Raval. Famous Ramblas pastry shop and café.
Casa Thomas C/Mallorca 291, Eixample. Browse designer furniture in a classic *modernista* building.
Hotel Espanya C/Sant Pau 9-11, El Raval. Have lunch in one of the city's most magnificent dining rooms.
Els Quatre Gats C/Montsio 3, Barri Gòtic. Mingle with the ghost of the young Picasso in Barcelona's original style bar.

with giant decorative lizards and a vast Hall of Columns, was originally conceived as a kind of "garden city" project for industrialist Eusebi Güell. Today, it's Barcelona's most high-profile park, also containing a small museum all about Gaudí's life and work. Gaudí also remodelled the Güell family's extraordinary downtown residence, the **Palau Güell**, which is found just off the famous Ramblas boulevard, and is open again now after long-term restoration.

All Gaudí's buildings and projects (and those of his lesser-known contemporaries) are accessible on an architectural route known as the **Ruta del Modernisme** (Ⓦwww.rutadelmodernisme.com), which comes with guidebook, discount vouchers and other special offers. A whole host of budget airlines compete on the Barcelona route with daily departures throughout the year from a dozen regional airports. For more help planning your trip see Ⓦwww.barcelonaturisme.com.

St Petersburg and the Hermitage

St Petersburg, Russia's second city, is Europe at its most gracious, an attempt by the eighteenth-century tsar Peter the Great to re-create the best of Western European elegance in what was then a far-flung outpost. Its position in the delta of the River Neva is unparalleled, full of watery vistas of huge and faded palaces. The city has not been revamped anywhere near as much as Moscow, and it preserves a unity of style and mood, and a stability lacking in the capital.

The two-hundred-metre long Baroque **Winter Palace** is the city's largest, most opulent palace. As loaded with history as it is with gilt and stucco, the palace was the official residence of the tsars – not to mention the court and 1500 servants. The main building was finished in 1762 and later new buildings were added to the east: the Small and Large Hermitages were added by Catherine the Great to enable her to be alone with her friends and her paintings, while the New Hermitage was launched as Russia's first public art museum in 1852. Beyond stands the Hermitage Theatre, Catherine the Great's private theatre, now used for concerts.

Together these buildings form one of the world's greatest museums, the **Hermitage** (®www.hermitagemuseum.org). Of awesome size and diversity, it embraces some three million objects, everything from ancient Scythian gold to Cubist art. After the state rooms and the Gold Collection, the most universally popular section is that covering modern European art from the nineteenth and twentieth centuries; it includes Matisse's wonderfully vibrant *The Dance*, a room full of Picassos, and vividly exotic Tahitian scenes by Gaugin. But it goes without saying that you'll need some help deciding what to see, as you can't possibly cover all the high points of the collection in one visit. The excellent Hermitage website can help with pre-planning, or take one of the **guided tours** aimed at assisting bewildered art-lovers. Overview tours focus on the more famous parts of the collection; theme tours cater for special interests, from Russian culture to Oriental art; and there's also a high-powered lecture series on an

White Nights

The most celebrated time to visit is during the famous **White Nights** of midsummer (mid-June to mid-July), when darkness never falls, but autumn and winter bathe the city in wonderful lighting effects and the city is much less crowded: apart from anything else, the locals are all out mushroom-hunting or skiing.

impressive range of topics, from Egyptology to Romanticism. Finally, special "conversation" tours allow you to engage with experts, whether you want to discuss the origins and meaning of art, Spanish painting or the construction of the Hermitage itself.

St Petersburg is not yet a fully fledged holiday destination – all the better, some might say. It does mean that flights tend to be with the major European airlines (rather than no-frills airlines), and packages are best arranged through a tour operator. There are also only a few tourist offices, none of them particularly useful. Instead, try Ⓦwww.saint-petersburg.com, which is full of city information and includes a hotel-booking service. Once there, most travellers use the **information desks** at their hotels, and there are English-language **newspapers**, such as the *St Petersburg Times*, and free magazines available at leading hotels.

City breaks

City breaks

Maastricht
Seville
Glasgow
Lisbon
Nice
Stockholm
Venice

Maastricht

Squashed between the Belgian and German borders, **Maastricht** is one of the most delightful cities in the Netherlands. A cosmopolitan place where three languages happily coexist, it's also one of the oldest towns in the country, with wonderful cobbled streets and lofty seventeenth-century houses. What's more, getting here is easy, with regular flights with Ryanair and KLM from London Stansted, or it's just a couple of hours on the train from Brussels. Go to ⓦwww.vvvmaastricht.nl for help booking accommodation in the city.

What to see and do

The busiest of Maastricht's many squares is **Markt**, at its most crowded during the Wednesday and Friday morning market. Otherwise, the pleasures lie chiefly in looking into the city's quiet churches and wandering the streets, stopping off for a coffee at Vrijthof, a grand open space flanked by a line of terrace cafés. This is a great place to take the pulse of the city, or you can take the short walk south down Bredestraat to another small, shady square crammed with café tables, where you'll find the Onze Lieve Vrouwe Basiliek, one of the city's major churches. On the other side of the square lies the appealing district of **Stokstraat Kwartier**, with narrow streets winding out to the fast-flowing River Jeker and the **Helpoort** fortress gateway of 1229. Head back to Vrijthof for some hearty Dutch fare in the evening – though the city also boasts a range of other restaurants, from French to Indonesian.

The next day you might consider a trip to the busy tourist town of **Valkenburg**, just outside the city, which provides a base for walking in the nearby hills and forests. Or there's a **wine trail** through the Jeker valley following a 10-kilometre-long vineyard walk (map available at the tourist office) – come in autumn and you might even see the locals hard at work grape-picking, which is probably not something you'd imagine encountering in the Netherlands.

When to go

You might want to time your visit to coincide with the city's **Fine Arts Fair** in early March (Ⓦwww.tefaf.com) – a fabulous opportunity to clap eyes on a jumble of Old Masters, modern art, European and Oriental ceramics, rare books, Classical antiquities and jewelled treasures before they're snapped up by museums and galleries.

Seville

Seville is the great city of the Spanish south and, provided you avoid the steamy summer months, you can have a lovely relaxed visit, exploring the historic latticework of narrow streets, patios and plazas, where minarets jostle for space among cupolas and palms. Ryanair, clickair, Iberia and British Airways all have regular flights to the city. The most attractive area to stay is the maze-like Barrio Santa Cruz near the cathedral; for help with accommodation and other practicalities, see Ⓦwww.turismo.sevilla.org or Ⓦwww.andalucia.org.

What to see and do

Your first port of call should be the **cathedral** (Ⓦwww.catedralsevilla.org), a structure of superlatives – the world's largest Gothic church, and third largest cathedral, with the world's largest altarpiece. Then stroll across Plaza del Triunfo to the **Alcázar**, a site that the rulers of Seville have occupied from the time of the Romans. Parts of the walls survive, but the palace was rebuilt in the fourteenth century by Pedro the Cruel whose works, some of the best surviving examples of Mudéjar architecture, form the nucleus of the Alcázar today. Take some time out and read a book in the rambling Alcázar gardens, or spend your siesta in the Plaza de España and adjoining María Luisa Park. (En route you pass the Fábrica de Tabacos, the old tobacco factory that was the setting for Bizet's Carmen, and today part of the university.)

Flamenco

Flamenco music and dance – more accurately known as *Sevillanas* – can be seen at dozens of places in the city, though many are tacky and overpriced. For authenticity, head to the rambling *La Carbonería* bar (c/Levías 18, northeast of Iglesia de San Juan), which often has spontaneous flamenco, or *Bar Casa Anselma* (c/Pages del Corro 49, Triana), where the dancing starts after 11.30pm. Alternatively, try the Triana *barrio*, home to a handful of flamenco academies, such as *Academia de Baile Manolo* (c/Rodrigo de Triana 30), where you can watch the students in action.

Save the afternoon for art, particularly the superb **Museo de Bellas Artes** on Plaza del Museo, housed in a beautiful former convent. Highlights include paintings by Murillo, as well as Zurbarán's *Carthusian Monks at Supper* and El Greco's portrait of his son. Across the river lies the **Triana** *barrio* that was once home to the city's gypsy community and is still a lively and atmospheric place. At Triana's northern edge is **La Cartuja**, a fourteenth-century former Carthusian monastery, and home to the **Museo del Arte Contemporáneo**, which displays work by local artists and hosts international exhibitions.

Come the evening, it's time to hit the city's numerous bars – a high concentration of them featuring barrelled **sherries** from nearby Jerez and Sanlúcar (the locals drink the cold, dry *fino*). In the centre of Santa Cruz a lively place is *Las Teresas* (c/Santa Teresa 2), while *Bodega Santa Cruz* (c/Rodrigo Caro) has a great atmosphere and tasty **tapas**. Another good choice, especially for fish tapas, is *Bar Modesto* (c/Cano y Cuento 5, by Avda. Menéndez Pelayo), in the northern corner of Santa Cruz. Or there's *Patio San Eloy* (c/San Eloy 9), a classic tiled warren serving fabulous small filled rolls.

When to go

Seville is quite simply magical in the early months of the year, warm and sunny and with hardly a tourist in sight. A wonderful seasonal sight – and scent – takes place in January and February, when the city's 20,000 **orange trees** burst into blossom. And if you want to see Seville in livelier mode, time your visit to coincide with one of the city's two great festivals – Easter's **Semana Santa** (or "Holy Week"), when up to a million visitors take to the streets around the cathedral, and the April **Feria**, which lasts for a week at the end of the month.

Glasgow

Glasgow is the largest city in Scotland, with Victorian architecture as grand as any in Britain. Chosen as European City of Culture in 1990, and City of Architecture and Design in 1999, Glasgow has broken the industrial shackles of the past and evolved into a city of stature and confidence – the local tourist authority bills it as "Scotland with style", which gives you an idea of how the contemporary city has positioned itself. It's easy to

Glasgow School of Art

The Botanic Gardens

If you're lucky enough to encounter some good weather when you're in Glasgow, take a trip to the West End and the lovely **Botanic Gardens** (@www.clyde-valley.com/Glasgow/botanic.htm), with their stately wrought-iron Victorian glasshouses. The largest of the glasshouses, Kibble Palace, is crammed with tree ferns and all manner of exotica, while back outdoors looping paths lead you through open parkland and past wonderfully profuse borders.

access, with GNER trains running up the east-coast route from London King's Cross, and Virgin Trains taking the western route from London Euston. For help **planning your trip**, go to @www.seeglasgow.com.

What to see and do

Stylish Glasgow is a magnet for art-lovers, and one of its most famous sons is the architect Charles Rennie Mackintosh, who had a major influence on the development of European Art Nouveau. Keen fans can buy a one-day **Mackintosh Trail** ticket (details on @www.crmsociety.com), though even with just a passing interest you won't want to miss the **Glasgow School of Art** at 167 Renfrew St (@www.gsa.ac.uk), a remarkable building that presents a fusion of Scottish manor-house solidity and modernist refinement. The interior, making maximum use of natural light, was also furnished and fitted entirely by the architect, and can be seen on a guided tour. If you've been intrigued by the art school, don't miss out on a cuppa and a scone at the Willow Tearooms (217 Sauchiehall Street), immaculately restored to the designs that Mackintosh made for the genteel Miss Cranston, the tearoom's original owner.

Glasgow's other grandstand attractions can easily take up a leisurely day or two – from the cathedral to Gallery of Modern Art – but to catch a glimpse of bygone days make your way to the **Tenement House**, 145 Buccleuch St (@www.nts.org.uk), an intriguing if sanitized vision of twentieth-century Glaswegian working-class life. With another half-day to spare, Pollok Country Park beckons, sited about four miles south of the centre, where the absorbing **Burrell Collection** (Ⓦwww.glasgowmuseums.com) is housed in a custom-built gallery – Sir William Burrell began collecting at the age of 15 and kept going until his death at 96, buying an average of two pieces a week, including works by Cézanne, Degas, Bellini and others, as well as an outstanding selection of Chinese ceramics, jades and bronzes.

It's a big city for **shopping**, whether along famous Sauchiehall Street (high-street shops, malls and department stores), in the elegant Princes Square Centre, or in the revamped eighteenth-century warehouses of Merchant City (boutiques and galleries). Glasgow has also acquired a great reputation for its **restaurants** in recent years; a long-standing favourite is *Café Gandolfi*, 64 Albion Street (Ⓦwww.cafegandolfi.com), an elegant bistro in Merchant City with rustic wooden furniture and a beautiful stained glass window depicting a shoal of fish. Nearby, on Blackfriars Street, *Babbity Bowster* is a lovely bistro-like pub with open fires, pared-down decor and some warming Scottish specialities such as Cullen Skink (thick haddock soup). For real old-style glamour eat at *Rogano* (Ⓦwww.roganoglasgow.com), a Glasgow legend with an impeccably stylish Art Deco interior and an irresistible oyster bar.

You can find innovative, challenging **theatre** at the Citizens' or Tramway theatres, both on the south side of the river, while the wonderful **Glasgow Film Theatre**, Rose Street (Ⓦwww.gft.org.uk), shows art films and old favourites.

When to go

Scotland isn't exactly famed for its climate, and you're likely to encounter lashing rain even in the height of summer. The best thing is to bring a brolly and forget the weather, timing your visit to coincide with one of the city's festivals. **Celtic Connections** (Ⓦwww.celticconnections.com) in January is a major music festival with a Celtic theme, or come for the **Glasgow International Jazz Festival** (Ⓦwww.jazzfest.co.uk) or **Glasgow River Festival** (both July).

Lisbon

There are few more immediately likeable European capitals than **Lisbon**. Set across seven hills above the River Tagus, it remains in some ways curiously provincial, rooted as much in the 1920s as the 2000s. Wooden trams clank up outrageous gradients past mosaic pavements, Art Nouveau cafés and the medieval quarter of Alfama, which hangs below the city's São Jorge castle. Nonetheless, there's been heavy investment in recent years, reclaiming rundown dockside areas and improving city-centre transport, so that today it combines an easy-going, human pace and scale with a vibrant, cosmopolitan identity. It's perfect for an unpressured mini break, but it's still something of a secret – go now before the crowds descend. There are daily flights with British Airways, easyJet, bmibaby, Monarch, TAP and others. City practicalities are all on Ⓦ www.visitlisboa.com.

What to see and do

A great way to get your bearings is to hop on board picture-book **tram #28**, Lisbon's most popular ride. The central section of its route runs from Rua da Conceição in the downtown Baixa area, past the Romanesque cathedral (Sé) and up towards the castle, rattling through some of Lisbon's steepest and narrowest streets – so close to the shop fronts you could almost take a can of sardines off the shelves.

Up at the castle there are sensational views over city and river, and then you can wind back down on foot to the Baixa, or lower town, where **Rossio** square is very much a focus for the city, with some great outdoor cafés. Then it's a short walk across and up to the **Chiado** district, which suffered much damage in a fire in 1988 but has been elegantly rebuilt by Portugal's premier architect Álvaro Siza Viera. It remains the city's most affluent quarter, centred on Rua Garrett and its fashionable shops and elegant cafés.

Afternoons can be spent uptown, perhaps taking time out at **Parque Eduardo VII**, whose big attraction is the Estufa Fria, a wonderful glasshouse filled with tropical plants and flamingo pools. Just north of here

Fado – the soundtrack of Lisbon

Fado is a mournful singing style somewhere between the blues and flamenco, but with roots in Brazil and the Portuguese colonies in Africa. It bemoans lost loves and better times, and while regular performances are held in established fado clubs in the Bairro Alto or Alfama, you might just find your best experience is stumbling upon a singer in a local bar or restaurant.

Adega do Ribatejo Rua do Diário de Notícias 23, Bairro Alto. Popular venue with a lower-than-usual minimum charge. Singers include a couple of professionals, the manager and even the cooks. Closed Sun.
O Senhor Vinho Rua do Meio a Lapa 18, Lapa. Famous club in the diplomatic quarter west of the centre, sporting some of the best fado singers in Portugal. Closed Sun.
A Severa Rua das Gáveas 51–61, Bairro Alto. A city institution featuring big names at big prices. Closed Thurs.

is the **Museu Calouste Gulbenkian** (®www.museu.gulbenkian.pt), the great museum of Portugal, divided into two distinct parts – the first devoted to Egyptian, Greco-Roman, Islamic and Oriental arts, the second to European. Meanwhile, down at the riverside suburb of Belém, an easy tram ride away from the centre, the major attraction is **Jerónimos** monastery, built in 1502 and still considered the city's finest monument.

You are spoiled for **restaurants** – for a start, there's an entire central street, Rua das Portas de Santo Antão, devoted to fish and seafood. The upper town quarter of Bairro Alto has the pick of the fashionable restaurants, bars and clubs – as well as the staid Port Wine Institute – or head for one of the revamped *docas* (docks) areas, where more trendy spots await. *Bica do Sapato* (®www.bicadosapato.com), for example, is part-owned by John Malkovich, and features a flash warehouse-style restaurant with upper-deck sushi bar.

When to go

Lisbon's main **festivals** are in June, especially those celebrating the so-called "Popular Saints", ie Anthony, John and Peter – these take over entire districts, complete with fireworks, barbecues, parades and music. You're best off avoiding the later summer months of July and August if possible, which can be very hot times to stroll around what is a very hilly city. Come in spring (as early as mid-February in Portugal) or autumn instead for some (usually) glorious weather and cheaper hotel prices.

Nice

Nice first grew into a major tourist resort in the nineteenth century, when large numbers of foreign visitors were drawn here by the agreeable Mediterranean climate. Add its beautiful location and attractive historical centre, and you still have the ingredients for a perfect break a century or so later. As capital of the French Riviera, the city also makes the best base for visiting the Riviera coast, which stretches for 30km, east to the Italian border and west to Cannes. You can get here easily with a whole host of airlines (including British Airways, Air France, Ryanair, EasyJet, Flybe, Jet2.com and bmibaby), though this is one European city break that you might equally do by train – you can book the entire journey from London with Eurostar, and the whole route takes around nine hours, door to door. Local practicalities are dealt with at Ⓦwww.nicetourism.com.

What to see and do

Start your day at the **Marché aux Fleurs**, lined with cafés, their tables spilling outdoors, perfect for an early coffee. A leisurely exploration of the city could continue at the chic **promenade des Anglais**, stretching along the pebble beach, laid out by nineteenth-century English residents to facilitate their afternoon stroll by the sea. The old town, **Vieux Nice**, is a rambling collection of narrow alleys lined with tall, rust-and-ochre

Exploring the Côte d'Azur

The **Côte d'Azur**, synonymous with glamour, wealth and luxury, is one of the prettiest and most built-up stretches of coast in the world. The coast's eastern reaches are its most spectacular, the mountains breaking their fall just a few metres before levelling off to the shore. **St-Tropez** is an expensive high spot, while at the opposite end of the coast, the vast, cosmopolitan sprawl of **Marseille** is quite different, with its big-city buzz and down-to-earth charm. July and August are the busiest months of the year, when accommodation can be hard to come by; and May can be equally hectic, with both **Monaco**'s Grand Prix and **Cannes**' Film Festival, pulling in the crowds.

houses, centred on Place Rossetti and the Baroque cathedral. Nearby is the entrance to the **Parc du Château** (there's an elevator and stairway by the Tour Bellanda, at the eastern end of Quai des États-Unis), decked out in a mock-Grecian style harking back to the original Greek settlement of Nikea. The point of climbing the stairs, apart from enjoying the perfumed greenery, is the view stretching west over the bay.

There are a couple of galleries that you won't want to miss, and both have lovely gardens. Overlooking the Roman baths in the upper suburb of Cimiez is the wonderful **Musée Matisse** (ⓦ www.musee-matisse-nice.org). Nice was the artist's home for much of his life, and the collection covers every period. Nearby, the uplifting **Musée Chagall** (ⓦ www.musee-chagall.fr) exhibits dazzlingly colourful Biblical paintings, stained glass and book illustrations.

Nice is a city that likes to stay up late, and it's not short of good restaurants and elegant bars. Sit outside at any of the places on Marché aux Fleurs for some old-town atmosphere, while if you want to try Niçois specialities, including great *socca* (a pancake made from chickpea flour), make for *Chez René Socca* (2 rue Miralhéti).

When to go

Nice enjoys an enviable Mediterranean climate, so the only time of year to avoid is the height of summer. **Carnival** (Feb or early March) packs out the town, with parades and music culminating at **Mardi Gras**, a city-wide party that takes up every street.

Stockholm

Stockholm comes lauded as Sweden's most beautiful city, and it lives up to its reputation. Built on fourteen islands, its tracts of water and range of monumental buildings give it an ageing, lived-in feel, quite at odds with its status as Sweden's most forward-looking city. Exploring it is easy – it might be the capital, but you can walk across the central area in under half an hour. Just watch out when you book your flights: Stockholm has three airports, though Stockholm Skavsta and Västerås (used by Ryanair) are both 100km from the capital, though they are linked to the city by connecting bus. The official visitors' guide is at ®www.stockholmtown.com, which has online accommodation reservations and other services.

What to see and do

Three islands – Riddarholmen, Staden and Helgeandsholmen – make up **Gamla Stan** (Old Stockholm), a clutter of seventeenth- and eighteenth-century Renaissance buildings, hairline medieval alleys and tall, dark houses whose intricate doorways still bear the arms of the wealthy merchants who once dwelled within. Principal building here is the **Storkyrkan**, consecrated in 1306 and technically Stockholm's cathedral – the monarchs of Sweden are married and crowned here. The Baroque interior is marvellous, with an animated fifteenth-century sculpture of St George and the Dragon, the royal pews, more like golden billowing thrones, and a monumental black and silver altarpiece.

Modern Stockholm lies just to the north of the old town, where the dis-

Stockholm made easy

You can't beat the **Stockholm Card** for taking the hassle out of sightseeing. Valid for 1, 2 or 3 days, it gives you free entry to 75 museums and attractions, free public transport and even sightseeing tours by boat. It's available at the Stockholm tourist office, or online from the official website, ⓦwww.stockholmtown.com.

trict of Norrmalm is characterized by **Kungsträdgården**, the most fashionable and central of the city's numerous parks; once royal gardens, they are now Stockholm's main meeting place and there's almost always something going on, especially in summer. Various museums stud the city – devoted to Swedish history and art, among others – but in the end it's the parks and outdoor spaces that really stand out. You could easily devote a whole day to wandering in the former royal hunting ground of **Djurgården**, for example, which is accessible by ferry. The TV tower here is one of Scandinavia's tallest structures, while if you were going to see just one museum there's a case for making it the extraordinary **Vasa Muséet** (ⓦwww.vasamuseet.se), which displays the Vasa warship which sank in Stockholm harbour after just twenty minutes of its maiden voyage in 1628. Walkways bring you nose to nose with the cannon hatches and restored decorative relief, exhibition halls display the retrieved bits and pieces, while films and videos explain the social and political life of the period – all with excellent English notes and regular English-language guided tours.

Stockholm is a highly cultured place with a year-round programme of concerts, including performances at the plush **Opera House** (ⓦwww.operan.se). The three main areas for decent eating in Stockholm, day or night, are Norrmalm, Gamla Stan and Södermalm. Many restaurants and hotels put out their tempting **smörgåsbord** at lunchtime, where you help yourself to unlimited portions of herring, smoked and fresh salmon, hot and cold meats, potatoes, salad, cheese and fruit. If the prospect of high Scandinavian prices worries you, it's worth knowing that most restaurants offer a set meal (the *dagens rätt*) at lunchtime – the best way to sample real Swedish cooking, including northern Swedish delicacies like reindeer and elk meat.

Stockholm

When to go

The **summer** in Sweden is short and rather frenetic, with the sun-starved locals extracting every ounce of pleasure they can from it – things reach a peak with the drunken Midsummer celebrations on June 21. It stays light until very late in July and August. September and late-May offer reasonable temperatures and a less hectic atmosphere, while the winter is long and dark.

Venice

The first-time visitor to **Venice** arrives with a heavy burden of expectations, most of them well founded. It is an extraordinarily beautiful city, and the major sights are all they are cracked up to be. You can make the journey part of the experience by taking the Orient Express train from London; otherwise, bmi, easyJet, Alitalia and British Airways fly from UK airports. See ⓦwww.turismovenezia.it and ⓦwww.comune.venezia.it for help with accommodation and other practicalities.

What to see and do

Everyone starts a tour of Venice with the incomparable **Piazza San Marco**, signalled from most parts of the city by the tall **Campanile** (bell-tower). Across the piazza, the **Basilica di San Marco** is the most exotic of Europe's cathedrals, modelled on Constantinople's Church of the Twelve Apostles, finished in 1094 and embellished over the succeeding centuries with trophies brought back from abroad. The mosaic above the doorway on the far left – *The Arrival of the Body of St Mark* – was made around 1260 and includes the oldest-known image of the basilica. Having explored the basilica, you can sit back and gaze at it from *Florian*, a beautiful historic café, or head to *Bar Paolin* on Campo Santo Stefano, reputed to make the best ice cream in Venice, with outside tables in one of the finest settings in the city.

Some of the finest architecture in Venice is in Dorsoduro, where you'll

Around Venice in style

One of the main pleasures in Venice is simply walking – slip down a side-street and you'll be amazed how the crowds melt away. If you want to take to the water, try one of the nippy **waterbuses** (*vaporetti*); tickets are available from most landing stages. A hot tip is that the gondola-style **traghetti** that cross the Canal Grande are a cheap way of having the gondola experience. Otherwise, **gondolas** themselves are pretty pricey: up to €100 for 45 minutes and an extra €100 for a singer. But – if you want the quintessential Venice trip – you may be prepared to fork out.

also find the wonderful **Galleria dell'Accademia**. This has one of the finest collections of European art, following the history of Venetian painting from the fourteenth to the eighteenth centuries. Five minutes' walk from the Accademia is the unfinished Palazzo Venier dei Leoni, home of the **Guggenheim Collection** (Ⓦ www.guggenheim-venice.it), and of Peggy Guggenheim for thirty years until her death in 1979. Her stunning private collection is an eclectic mix of pieces from her favourite modernist movements and artists, including works by Brancusi, De Chirico, Max Ernst and Malevich.

After a day's sightseeing, make for legendary *Harry's Bar* in San Marco, the best spot in town to sip a **cocktail**. The next day you might want to head further afield, where Venice's other islands offer some interesting shopping opportunities. **Murano** is chiefly known for glass-blowing, while the nearby island of **Burano** is still largely a fishing community, but with a thriving trade in lace-making.

When to go

The most famous annual event is **Carnevale** (Ⓦ www.visitvenice.co.uk/venice-carnival.html), which occupies the ten days leading up to Lent, finishing on Shrove Tuesday with a masked ball, dancing in the Piazza, street parties, plus pageants and performances. Avoid the city in high summer, when it is overrun with visitors.

Culture

Culture

Book-browsing in Hay-on-Wye
Mozart week in Salzburg
Writing courses in Ireland
Berlinale, Berlin's film festival
Ball season in Vienna
Fasnacht in Luzern
Kraków's Jewish heritage

Book-browsing in Hay-on-Wye

To the north of the Black Mountains, just on the Welsh side of the border with England, is the small town of **Hay-on-Wye** (ⓦwww.hay-on-wye.co.uk), famous as the second-hand book capital of the world – it might only have a population of a couple of thousand but it boasts at least thirty major bookshops, mainly selling second-hand titles as well as intriguing memorabilia such as Victorian *cartes de visite*. Whether you're looking for some light holiday reading or a rare Jane Austen first edition, this is the place to start your search. The town's other claim to fame is that one of its booksellers, Richard George William Pitt Booth, declared the town a kingdom and himself its ruler in 1977, on the significant date of April 1. The claims boosted the town's popularity, and this and the emergent **Hay Festival** (ⓦwww.hayfestival.com) put it firmly on the map.

Indeed, the literary festival, held in May/June, has gone from strength to strength – nowadays it draws a staggering 80,000 people for its ten days of readings, book launches, author Q&As and general literary junketing. Bill Clinton went so far as to call it "the Woodstock of the mind". You'll need to book well in advance to hear the likes of Martin Amis and Doris Lessing talk about their work, while figures from the film world and politics like Cate Blanchett and Al Gore all make appearances. There's also a full film programme, DJs and theatre, stand-up comedy, music events and even an on-site circus. Indeed, the festival has got so big that, like Edinburgh, it has grown a **fringe** (ⓦwww.hayfringe.co.uk), which features smaller, alternative book-related events and readings.

Fun as the festival is, it rather overwhelms the character of this charming little place – much of the pleasure of being in Hay is in quiet book-browsing, and exploring the surroundings. Paths along the rushing Wye river soon lead you out of the town and into some gloriously lush countryside.

Hay directory

Baskerville Hall ⓦ www.baskervillehall.co.uk. A rambling Victorian country house where Conan Doyle was a frequent visitor – you can stay here and the hall is sometimes used as a festival venue.

Boz Books ⓦ www.bozbooks.demon.co.uk. This second-hand bookshop on Castle Street specializes in nineteenth-century literature – there's always a good selection of first editions by Dickens.

Free Rein ⓦ www.free-rein.co.uk. Unescorted horseback tours through the Cambrian Mountains; you stay at equine-friendly farms and inns where they feed the horse and provide you with a packed lunch for the next day.

Hay Cinema Bookshop ⓦ www.haycinemabookshop.co.uk. Not a bookshop about cinema, but a bookshop in a cinema – it was established in 1965 and carries 200,000 titles on a huge range of topics.

Hay-on-Wye ⓦ www.hay-on-wye.co.uk. The town's official website, invaluable for booking accommodation, especially for the festival, when you'll have to arrange things well in advance.

Marches Walks ⓦ www.marches-walks.co.uk. Guided walks in the Black Mountains, the Brecon Beacons, or the gentler Wye Valley.

The Three Tuns ⓦ www.three-tuns.com. Hay's oldest pub, located in a characterful sixteenth-century building.

Mozart week in Salzburg

You can hardly avoid **Salzburg**'s most famous son, Wolfgang Amadeus Mozart, whose bright-eyed visage peers from every box of the city's ubiquitous chocolate delicacy, the *Mozartkugeln*. And around the time of his birthday each year, on January 27, Salzburg really pulls out the stops with **Mozart week** (Mozartwoche), a series of concerts by prestigious soloists, ensembles and orchestras. It's acknowledged as one of the most important classical music events in Europe, where you are likely to hear concerts by the Viennese Philharmonic and the Camerata Salzburg, as well as performances by internationally known singers. In 2007 the festival branched out with contemporary works by John Cage and Pierre Boulez, while

A short walk with Mozart

Start your walk with Mozart at the central **Mozartplatz**, home to a statue of the composer and overlooked by the **Glockenspiel**, a seventeenth-century musical clock whose chimes attract crowds at 7am, 11am and 6pm. A short stroll to the east is the canary-yellow **Mozarts Geburtshaus** (Ⓦwww.mozarteum.at), where the musical prodigy was born (in 1756) and lived till the age of 17. It is an evocative place, housing some fascinating period instruments, including a baby-sized violin used by Wolfgang Amadeus as a child. After time out for a coffee in one of Salzburg's most renowned cafés, the elegant *Tomasselli* (Alter Markt 9), you can cross the river for Makartplatz, where you'll find **Mozarts Wohnhaus**, the family home from 1773 to 1787, containing an engrossing multimedia history of the composer and his times.

there was also a programming strand devoted to Mozart's interpretation of other composers' works, along with premieres of entirely new works. Performances are held across the city in some dramatic settings – coming out of Salzburg Castle, after a Mozart concert, and seeing the lights of the city spread out below you is one of Europe's great delights.

The city is easy to reach, with flights from UK airports on Flybe and Jet2.com among others. Check out Ⓦwww.salzburginfo.at for accommodation options in the city and, if you hanker after a bit of light relief, don't miss Panorama's Sound of Music tour (Ⓦwww.panoramatours.com) – the hills are still alive with music, forty-odd years after the film was shot in and around the city.

Writing courses in Ireland

If you've always longed to let your literary side come to the fore, a writing course is a great way to equip you with the relevant skills and give you time to explore your ideas. **Ireland**, with its rich literary heritage, excels

Dublin's theatre

Dublin rich literary heritage extends to the theatre: the world-famous Abbey featured Yeats, J.M. Synge and Sean O'Casey as house playwrights, and the city's three playhouses continue a vibrant tradition of theatrical innovation.

Abbey Theatre Ⓦ www.abbeytheatre.ie. Founded in 1904 by W.B. Yeats and Lady Gregory. The building also contains the Peacock Theatre, which stages experimental shows.

Gate Theatre Ⓦ www.gatetheatre.ie. Another of Dublin's literary institutions, staging classic and modern Irish theatre.

Project Ⓦ www.project.ie. This long-standing arts venue continues to mount experimental and politically sensitive theatre.

in such courses: established writers will critique your work, and being in a group of aspiring authors is also a terrific opportunity to share ideas and inspiration. This being Ireland, you'll never be far from a cosy pub where you can discuss plotlines with your new pals.

The two organizations listed below give a real taster for this varied country, as well as being renowned for the quality of their courses. The first is in **Dublin** (Ⓦ www.visitdublin.com), a splendidly monumental city with some unparallelled Georgian architecture and a famously lively atmosphere. If you're low on inspiration, the **Dublin Writers Museum** on Parnell Square (Ⓦ www.writersmuseum.com) whisks you through Irish literary history from early Christian writings up to Samuel Beckett. Two blocks east of here, at 35 North Great George's St, the **James Joyce Centre** (Ⓦ www.jamesjoyce.ie) runs intriguing walking tours of the novelist's Dublin haunts (current details are on the website), while a night at the theatre (see box) might just inspire you further.

In the southwest of Ireland, the **Dingle Peninsula** (Ⓦ www.dingle-peninsula.ie) is a place of intense, shifting beauty, with spectacular mountains, long sandy beaches and the splinter-slatted mass of rocks that defines the extraordinary coast at Slea Head. Here is one of the greatest concentrations of Celtic ruins in Ireland, while the now uninhabited Blasket Islands once generated a wealth of Irish literature.

Writing courses

Dingle Writing Courses ⓦ www.dinglewritingcourses.ie. Weekend courses are held in the residential centre at Inch on the Dingle Peninsula in County Kerry – expect writing exercises, one-to-one tuition, group projects and time to yourself. Past classes have included poetry, fiction, scriptwriting, memoir and a special course on the literary story of the Blasket Islands. There's tasty home-cooked food to fuel your endeavours, and the views of Kerry Strand, three miles of white sandbar, should provide you with some inspiration. From €350.

The Irish Writers Centre ⓦ www.writerscentre.ie. High-profile writers lead weekend and five-day courses in Dublin on fiction, non-fiction, poetry and getting published. One-day master classes are led by literary stars such as Roddy Doyle, Edna O'Brien and Will Self, and you can pop into the centre for the "Out to Lunch" poetry series, featuring established and emerging poets giving free readings. From €200.

Berlinale, Berlin's film festival

Energetic and irreverent, **Berlin** is a welcoming city where the speed of change in the past few years has been astounding. After the Wall fell in 1989, Berlin's status as national capital was confirmed. These days, parliament sits in the renovated Reichstag (Bundestag), and some of the city's excellent museum collections have been put back together again, housed in buildings at the forefront of architectural design.

The revived national capital has become a magnet for film-makers, artists and musicians, particularly in February with the ten-day **Berlinale** film festival (ⓦ www.berlinale.de) which, unlike the more famous one in Cannes, is geared towards the general public. Coming up for its 60th year, the festival is firmly established on the international scene, and shows a staggering 350 films, most of them European or international premieres.

You'll see large-scale international movies in the competition; inde-

The Berlin Film Museum

Don't miss the **Berlin Film Museum** (@www.filmmuseum-berlin.de) while you're in town. It's located in the Sony Center at Potsdamer Strasse 2, a futuristic edifice designed by German-American architect Helmut Jahn. The permanent collection takes you from German silents via Nazi propaganda pictures to post-war and contemporary movies, with set models from classics such as *Metropolis* and *The Blue Angel*. There's a special section on homegrown goddess Marlene Dietrich, featuring some of her glamorous costumes and the huge metal cases required to hold her luggage. Finally, you can stock up on postcards, Deitrich memorabilia and weighty tomes at the bookshop.

pendent and art-house productions in the "Panorama" strand; movies for young people in the "Generation" section; vibrant German cinema productions in "Perspektive Deutsches Kino"; and experimental and world cinema in the "International Forum of New Cinema". Then there's an annual "Homage", which focuses on one of cinema's greats – Anouk Aimée and American director Arthur Penn have been honoured in recent years. Finally no film festival is complete without prizes – the much coveted golden and silver Bears.

To get to the city, either hop on the overnight Brussels–Berlin train, or fly with easyJet, Ryanair, Jet2.com, Air Berlin or British Airways. For help planning your trip see @www.berlin-tourism.de, the official site of the city's tourist office. There's an invaluable guide in English, *New Berlin Magazine* (@www.newberlinmagazine.com), together with its listings supplement, the *New Berlin Weekly* (@www.newberlinmagazine.com).

Ball season in Vienna

Most people visit **Vienna** with a vivid image in their minds: a romantic place full of Habsburg nostalgia and musical resonances. And, to be fair, it's unlikely to disappoint, with its eclectic feast of architectural styles, from High Baroque through to the monumental imperial projects of the late-nineteenth century. In keeping with the old-world style, the winter months are given over to public balls: spectacular events which are very much part of the calendar of the waltzing locals, but which also welcome visitors who are keen to join in. There's useful general information on the official city (Ⓦwww.wienerzeitung.at) and tourist authority (Ⓦwww.wien.info) websites, though for specific ball information check the list of useful contacts below.

There are a staggering 150 **balls** staged in Vienna in the early months of the year, in venues ranging from humble church halls to the Imperial Palace. The proceedings are pretty formal, with a fanfare on arrival, string orchestras, halls decked with thousands of flowers and formal dress *de rigeur* – black tie for men and ball gowns for women. The dances range from waltzes to quicksteps, polkas to tangos, and some previous dance ex-

Vienna

Viennese café culture

Most cafés, particularly those dubbed *Café-Konditorei*, or *Kaffee-Konditorei*, offer a tempting array of freshly baked Austrian cakes and pastries. *Apfelstrudel* is apple and raisins wrapped in pastry and topped with icing sugar. *Mohnstrudel* has a poppyseed and raisin filling. *Topfenstrudel* has a sweet curd cheese filling while *Linzertorte* is a jam tart with almond pastry and *Sachertorte* a famously rich chocolate cake.

Central 1, Herrengasse 14. Traditional meeting place of Vienna's intelligentsia, and Trotsky's favourite Kaffehaus – this is probably the most ornate of Vienna's cafés. Closed Sun eve.

Demel 1, Kohlmarkt 14. Vienna's most prestigious café.

Landtmann 1, Dr-Karl-Lueger-Ring 4. A favourite with Freud and Marlene Dietrich, though today's clientele is a mixture of politicians, actors, regulars and tourists.

Sperl 6, Gumpendorferstr. 11. The fin-de-siècle interior is one of the finest in the city. July & Aug closed Sun.

Una 7, Museumsplatz 1. Best of the Museums Quartier cafés, with a wonderful vaulted floral ceramic ceiling, an imaginative menu and a friendly vibe. Closed Sun eve.

perience is required to make it a truly enjoyable experience – though the copious amounts of champagne on offer should help to break down any inhibitions you may have. At least a third of the locals attend a ball during any one season, and they're really lively events, usually lasting until two or three in the morning. Indeed, many people stay up long enough to hit one of the city's glamorous cafés (see box) come the morning. To buy tickets, see the links on Ⓦwww.ballkalender.info.

As far as getting to the city goes, if you want the leisurely option then the train from London takes under twenty hours. Otherwise, fly with Air Berlin or Niki.

Useful contacts

ⓦ **www.ballkalender.info** Published in November by the Vienna tourist office, this is the all-important calendar of the ball season.

ⓦ **www.costumier.com** A Viennese family business (since 1862) where you can hire suitable ball garb.

ⓦ **www.waltzballs.org/vienna.html** A handy site with lots of information on ball etiquette.

Fasnacht in Lucerne

An hour south of Basel and Zürich is the beautiful Swiss city of **Lucerne** (ⓦwww.luzern.org), offering captivating mountain views, lake cruises and a picturesque old-town medieval quarter. But Lucerne is no museum piece; people love their café culture here, and the whole city erupts in March or April in celebration of the pre-Lenten blow-out known as **Fasnacht**.

Lucerne

This is the Swiss take on Mardi Gras and it is definitely at the livelier end of the spectrum – it's an event where it's impossible merely to spectate. The marching bands prepare their floats and costumes months in advance, but the six-day festivities officially begin at 5am on "**Dirty Thursday**", with the costumed figure of legendary folk character Fritschi leaning out of a window in the Rathaus (city hall): a cannon sounds and the party starts, with oompah bands, acrobats and revellers taking over the streets. The next three days see more parties and general merry-making, and on "**Fat Monday**" strolling musicians and *commedia dell'arte* players in colourful masks bring an element of pantomime to the proceedings. The Old Town is taken over by masked dances in the evening, broadcast live on Swiss TV. Tuesday is **Mardi Gras** itself, when all the bands perform together al fresco, and the eating, drinking and dancing goes on until the early hours. By morning on the Wednesday, an altogether more Swiss sense of sobriety returns.

Speedy Swiss trains make the train journey to Lucerne a pleasure; to fly you'll need to travel to Zürich, Geneva or Basel and take a connecting train from there – all the details are on the Swiss Federal railways' website ⓦwww.sbb.ch.

Kraków's Jewish heritage

Kraków is perhaps *the* architectural gem of Central Europe and Poland's intellectual heart. Its assembly of monuments has been listed by UNESCO as one of the world's most significant historic sites, and the Old Town retains an atmosphere of fin-de-siècle stateliness, the streets a cavalcade of churches and palaces. It's now pretty well known as a city-break destination, especially by the younger crowd who have made it something of an arty, party destination. But there's so much more to it than bars and nightlife, not least its rich Jewish heritage, which provides a gripping cultural reason for a visit. British Airways, easyJet and Jet2.com all have regular flights to the city, and once there you can make use of the information on

Klezmer music

You can further explore Kraków's Jewish heritage by listening to **klezmer music**, immediately identifiable by its pacy and expressive tunes. Characteristic instruments are the violin, clarinet, accordion and trombone, which laugh and cry in a deliberate imitation of the human voice. The best places to head to hear *klezmer* are the city's Jewish restaurants in Kazimierz, such as lively *Arka Noego* at ul. Szeroka 2.

the websites ⓦwww.krakow.pl and ⓦwww.inyourpocket.com, the latter the site of the reliable English-language city-guide *Kraków in Your Pocket*.

The **Kazimierz** district became Kraków's Jewish quarter as early as 1495; it grew to become one of the main centres of Polish Jewry, but in March 1941 the entire Jewish population of the city was crammed into a tiny ghetto over the river. Waves of deportations to the concentration camps followed and the ghetto was finally liquidated in March 1943, ending seven centuries of Jewish life in Kraków. Today Kazimierz is a fashionable and bohemian residential district, with much to see and plenty of interesting shops, cafés and bars. The tiny **Remu'h Synagogue** at ul. Szeroka 40 is one of two still functioning in the quarter. The tombstones of its cemetery were buried and therefore largely saved from Nazi ransacking. Fragments are collaged together to form an impressive wall just inside the entrance. The **Old Synagogue**, at ul. Szeroka 24, is the oldest surviving Jewish religious building in Poland. Since the war it's been carefully restored and turned into a **Museum of Kraków Jewry**, including a permanent exhibition of traditional art by Polish Jews. One block to the southeast, at ul. Dajwór 18, the **Galicia Jewish Museum** displays a memorable series of photographs evoking the way rural Poland's Jewish heritage has been neglected; there's also a good bookstore, and concerts and lectures are frequently held here. Another interesting visit is the **Synagoga Izaaka** (Isaac Synagogue), at ul. Kupa 18, which presents photographs and short silent films illustrating the life of Kazimierz Jews before and during the war.

Food and drink

Food and drink

Regional cooking in Tuscany and Umbria

Bruges, beer and chocolate

Porto and the Douro wine route

Cordon Bleu Paris

Whisky tasting in Scotland

Tapas in Madrid

Regional cooking in Tuscany and Umbria

The Italian heartland of **Tuscany** represents the archetypal image of the country – its walled towns and vineyard-covered slopes the classic backdrops to Renaissance art – while to the east lie the rolling hills, woods and valleys of **Umbria**. These remain deeply rural regions that for the most part have resisted large-scale agriculture: villagers still grow their own vegetables, hunting is a common pastime, and the local vines produce some of the greatest wines in Italy. Local delicacies – black Norcia truffles, chestnuts and wild berries, creamy pecorino cheese and delicate olive oils – are treated with the utmost reverence. But despite the respectful approach, there's fun to be had – learning about the region's cuisine is not nearly as daunting as skimming sauces in Paris. But you can still acquire some real skills, such as hand-making gnocchi and pasta, baking focaccia and pairing your dinner with the right wine.

The listings below give a taster of both regions, from the buzzy urban centre of Florence to remote Umbrian farmhouses. And when school's out, you can relax with a dip in the pool or a nose around the local market. You'll have to make your own travel arrangements to the region but with daily flights to Florence, Pisa and Perugia from UK airports that's not a problem.

Cookery schools

Casa Ombuto Ⓦ www.italiancookerycourse.com. Hosts Michele and Carla adopt a leisurely approach – classes in the cantina of their villa in the Tuscan hills south of Florence don't start till 3pm. The course lasts for seven days, with plenty of time for swimming in their beautiful pool and walking near the villa as well as rustling up four-course Italian meals – everything from *crostini* to wild boar with polenta. There's also a day excursion which takes in visits to a salami factory, pecorino and goat's cheese farm, and an olive oil mill. From £1420.

Divina Cucina Ⓦ www.divinacucina.com. Self-styled diva Judy Witts Francini runs one-, two- and three-day classes from her cooking studio near the central market in

Olive oils, Tuscany

Florence. You'll tour the market with her, sampling the best of the produce on offer, and learn to wine-pair with a sommelier. Each class then produces a genuine Tuscan meal, from starter to dessert. From £200.

Organic Tuscany ⓦ www.organictuscany.org. Shilpa and Riccardo, whose home is near the medieval town of Certaldo, have a holistic approach, taking guests to organic farms as well as to vineyards and oil presses. Two of the 7-night courses are vegetarian; others are vegetarian-friendly. Learn to stir the perfect risotto, create light *sformati* (vegetable flans) and assemble pizzas for the wood-fired oven. You can also explore nearby San Gimignano, Florence and Siena – the hosts can provide hiking maps – while accommodation is in self-catering apartments in villas and farmhouses, all with access to a pool. From £815.

Tuscan Women Cook ⓦ www.tuscanwomencook.com. Guests stay in the village of Montefollonico, where the expert tutors are local Tuscan women. This is a great chance to improve your language skills as the cooks teach in Italian which is translated for you. Classes are hands-on round the farmhouse table, and you won't leave without being able to make excellent handmade pasta. Visits to markets and food festivals are included, as well as advice from the local wine master and trips to nearby restaurants. From £1730.

umbriacooks4u ⓦ www.umbriacooks4u.com. This is a good flexible option – classes are either taken in the elegant home of the tutor, Tita, located ten minutes from

pro·age | Dove

Feeling better than ever before

Mature women today are part of a new generation, living life to the full. They are more socially active, financially independent and physically fitter than their mothers' generation.

Indeed the majority of UK women consider themselves too young to be old and are proud to celebrate their age*.

Travelling and experiencing new things are a top priority for many mature women. As a result, we've asked a selection of real women from our ProAge campaign to give us their views on the best getaways in Europe and provide some handy tips for making the most of your time away...

* Research carried out by Dove – September 2006

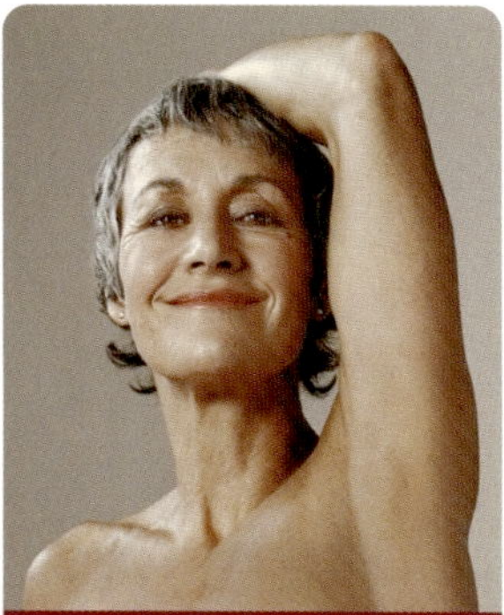

Kate Harrison, 54

San Sebastián is such an elegant city – with a beautiful, long beach promenade, busy port, great shops and a stunning rocky coastline. Now that my family have grown up it's easier to travel and I'm anxious to start exploring more. When the children were young I had to think of holidays which would appeal to them and fall within the family budget. Now there are only two of us, my husband and I can please ourselves. We like to make the most of an area and try to get a feel for the place, visiting old buildings, museums and exploring the countryside.

Weekend hotspot:

SAN SEBASTIÁN, SPAIN

"I love sitting under a coloured awning watching the Spanish way of life go by..."

Top travel tip: Don't pack too much – go for several tops to wear with one skirt and a pair of trousers. Pack a comfortable pair of shoes for sightseeing – I take sandals or trainers. And roll clothes up together so they don't crease!

Top travel beauty tip: To keep fresh on the move I like to pack a Dove ProAge deodorant in my handbag. Dove ProAge Roll-On Deodorant, rrp £1.69

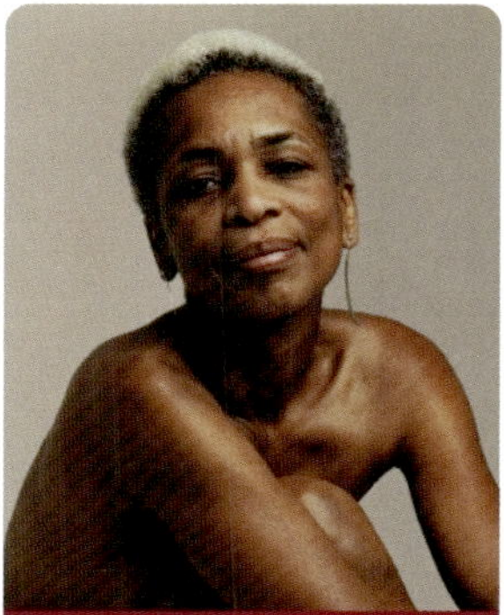

Diana Harwood Baynes, 57

Weekend hotspot:

PARIS, FRANCE

Paris, I love Paris, if only for its desire to create and maintain beauty. I love the uniformity of the trees along the Champs-Élysées, the majesty of the Arc de Triomphe and the bravery of the glass pyramid outside the Louvre Museum. I love the risks the Parisians are prepared to take with architecture. The Pompidou Centre was exciting and innovative when built in the 70s and still draws my attention today. Somehow wine, coffee and croissants taste better there and the French artistry with food, though somewhat rich at times, can be magical and one of the joys of living.

"Visiting places is so much more exciting when you are feeling alive and ready to experience!"

Top travel tip: It has always been my aim to reduce my luggage to a toothbrush and a pair of knickers. I haven't quite managed it yet but it is still an ambition. Just think how liberating travel would be if we didn't have to carry anything.

Top travel beauty tip: I always use a body wash such as Dove ProAge to help my skin's natural cell renewal. A beautiful broad-brimmed hat and sunglasses are also a must for any sunny location. Dove ProAge Beauty Body Wash, rrp £2.99

I spent a wonderful weekend in Paris last year. It was soon after I met my boyfriend and we spent ages wandering around the stylish shops of the Jewish Rue de Rosier, getting lost in the quirky, mysterious cobbled streets. Try cosying up at a terrace coffee shop on the Champs-Élysées and do some people watching. Don't forget your camera: the light is a photographer's dream. Sample the food stalls at Rue Mouffetard. The quaint market is a visual treat with glorious colours and arrangements of cheese, saucissons, nuts and chocolates. Trying a few delicacies is a sensual gastronomic experience for the soul.

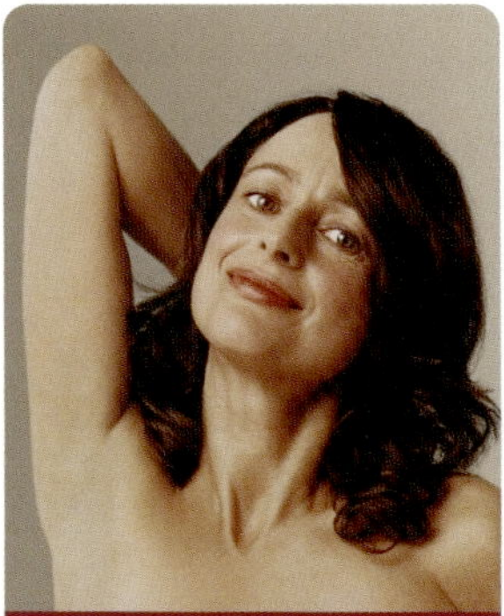

Jane Allen, 52

Weekend hotspot:

PARIS, FRANCE

"The beauty and magnificence of the architecture is incredible..."

Top travel tip: 'Feel the culture', and look out for where the locals eat. This guarantees authentic food at the best prices. Also rather than paying over the odds for room service, buy your own champagne from the local supermarket and if you don't have a fridge just chill your champers in the sink!

Top travel beauty tip: Whenever I pack my bag I always remember to slip in my Dove ProAge deodorant, to guarantee a cool, calm, fresh arrival. Dove ProAge Aerosol Deodorant, rrp £2.49

Barbara Field, 57

You can fly to Nice in the wee hours of Friday and return late Sunday night. I don't stay in Nice but rent a car and go to a friend's small, wonderful villa in the hills near Fréjus. Then I do nothing, except read and absorb the warm air outside.

"Then I do nothing, except read and absorb the warm air outside..."

Weekend hotspot:

FRÉJUS NEAR NICE, FRANCE

Top travel tip: Never leave home without good books and a new notebook to write in. I never forget my mini Sony tape recorder so I can record my dreams in that luscious space between 'asleep' and 'awake'. Wherever we are, we live whole lives at night, I record them before they vanish. I am a rubbish packer and always forget things, but I like to go places where it really doesn't matter.

Top travel beauty tip: I pack my ProAge shampoo to ensure my hair stays thick and full. For days when I decide not to wash my hair I use my Ayurvedic hair oil to keep my locks shiny. Dove ProAge Shampoo, rrp £2.59

Michele Clement Dubois, 54

Weekend hotspot:

STE-FOY-EN-TARENTAISE, FRENCH ALPS

My favourite destination is a hamlet of twenty buildings, situated close to Ste-Foy-en-Tarentaise in the French Alps. At 1600 metres, it has the most awesome view across a ravine to the glacier opposite. My favourite memory is being awakened by the sound of cow-bells just before dawn, sitting up in bed and watching the sun rise and hit the peak of the glacier. Alpine flowers, most predominantly orchids of which there are literally millions, litter the meadows. All this – the piercing clarity by day, long mountain walks, spectacular views at every turn, roaring log fires in the evening and, naturally, a glass of Chablis in the sauna – make it one of the most memorable, energizing and revitalising experiences imaginable. Pure magic!

"There's no telephone, just the sound of rushing streams flowing down to the Isere river thousands of feet below..."

Top travel tip: Make sure you pack appropriate shoes, a small backpack containing a camera (to capture the magic), a notebook and pencils/pen, water and sun cream.

Top travel beauty tip: My hair is naturally curly and prone to dryness, so a serum or conditioner and a diffuser work for me. ProAge Conditioner, rrp £2.59

Barcelona is full of wonderful architectural contrast and I love it. I've always enjoyed travelling and experiencing different cultures and lifestyles. However, travel is so much more relaxing now the children have grown up. I can visit the tourist attractions I want to see without having to worry about them. This new found freedom means I can really enjoy a city – of course I do still miss them!

"You are surrounded by art and a beach, what more could you want?"

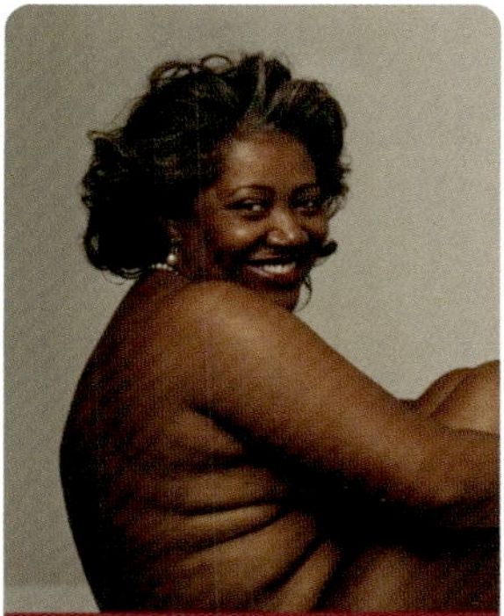

Mirinette Morrison, 54

Weekend hotspot:

BARCELONA, SPAIN

Top travel tip: Learn a few simple phrases like 'goodbye', 'hello' and 'thank you'. It pays to put in the effort and express an interest in the country, culture and language.

Top travel beauty tip: Moisturise, moisturise, moisturise from your head to your toes! I do this every day to leave my skin feeling refreshed, replenished and ready for the next adventure.

Dove ProAge Beauty Body Lotion, rrp £4.99

Dove ProAge Body Cream Oil, rrp £4.99

Looking after me

No matter what our age, we all want to feel the best we possibly can.

Dove ProAge is a skin and hair care range designed to meet the unique beauty needs of mature women. Each of the products are specifically formulated to give more mature skin and hair what it needs right now.

The Dove ProAge suitcase essentials:

PROAGE HAND CREAM contains AHAs to help remove dead cells, smoothing the appearance of wrinkles, age spots and uneven skin tone, rrp £2.29

PROAGE BODY CREAM OIL designed for very dry skin, contains glycerine and olive oil, rrp £4.99

PROAGE BEAUTY BODY LOTION designed for normal skin, with AHAs and glycerine to give dull, tired skin a luminous, healthy glow, rrp £4.99

PROAGE NECK & CHEST BEAUTY SERUM smooths the appearance of fine lines and wrinkles in these delicate areas, rrp £6.99

PROAGE BEAUTY BODY WASH helps to maintain hydration levels in the skin with natural oil and gentle Dove cleansers to care for your skin, rrp £2.99

PROAGE ANTI-PERSPIRANT DEODORANTS provide 24-hour protection from odour and wetness. With a quarter moisturising cream, ProAge helps nourish skin and keep underarms in optimum condition. Aerosol, rrp £2.49 / Roll-on, rrp £1.69

PROAGE SHAMPOO contains gentle cleansing agents that create volume from root to tip by removing the build-up that weighs hair down, rrp £2.59

PROAGE CONDITIONER helps protect brittle hair against daily damage, rrp £2.59

Taking it easy: the Slow Food movement

Slow Food is an eco-friendly gastronomic organization that originated in Italy but has developed into a world-wide phenomenon. After all, who could resist its goal is to promote "sensual pleasure and slow, long-lasting enjoyment"? Part-pressure group, part research institute and part social club, Slow Food now has 80,000 members who form 850 local groups known as *convivia*. Their activities focus on fun forms of education, from visits to local orchards to talks by enthusiastic food experts. They also help children to understand the link between the seasons and what appears on their plates – for example, each local group must create a school garden as part of its activities. The movement, with a little snail as its logo, continues to grow at a very un-snail-like pace.

stunning hilltop Perugia, or in your own holiday rental apartment or villa. These are one-day courses, where you will learn to rustle up several appetisers, two first courses and a second meat course. Umbrian wine and two desserts round off a fun learning experience. From €120.

Vallicorte ⓦwww.vallicorte.com. Well-organized courses that attempt to match groups in terms of age and language, with accommodation at a wonderful old villa surrounded by olive groves, located twenty minutes' drive from the medieval walled town of Lucca. Classes are held in the barn/cookery school and after the morning session you have lunch and a snooze, followed by classes in the afternoon. From €65 per day, excluding accommodation.

Bruges, beer and chocolate

Bruges' reputation as one of the most perfectly preserved medieval cities in Europe has made it the most popular tourist destination in Belgium. This is an unmissable place – its intimate, winding streets, narrow canals and ancient buildings live up to even the most inflated hype. And it's a must for art-lovers: the Groeninge Museum houses a superb sample of Flemish paintings, including several by Jan van Eyck, who lived and worked in Bruges from 1430 until his death eleven years later; while the old chapel of St Jans Hospitaal displays an exquisite collection of paintings by Hans Memling, who spent most of his working life in the city.

In short, Bruges is a great little place in which to unwind, particularly out of season, when the streets, shops and galleries don't seem quite as busy. It also offers some great indulgence opportunities, whether you decide to explore the varied wonders of Belgian beer or go for some serious chocolate therapy. You could even combine the two – let's not forget that this is the country that created a chocolate beer.

For help with Bruges travel practicalities, consult ⓦwww.brugge.be, ⓦwww.visitbelgium.com and ⓦwww.visitflanders.com. Getting here is a breeze, with regular trains from Brussels that take just an hour and connect with the whizzy Eurostar service from St Pancras International. There are also ferries from Dover and Calais to nearby Zeebrugge, and frequent flights from regional UK airports to Brussels.

Beer

Don't like beer? Then think again, since Belgium takes the humble tipple and adds a dollop of class. The most common brands are Stella Artois, Jupiler and Maes, but this merely scratches the surface. In total, there are about 700 speciality beers made in the country, from dark stouts to fruit beers, wheat beers to caramel-like ales – something, in fact, to suit any palate. The most famous are probably the strong ales brewed by the country's five Trappist monasteries, of which the most widely available is Chimay. Like fine wines, each beer requires its own specially shaped glass and should be sipped and savoured, whether in a sophisticated city café or over a quiet dinner – you'll never look at lager in the same light again.

Brewery tours in Bruges can be made at De Halve Maan (Verbrand Nieuwland 10; ⓦwww.halvemaan.be), a family concern in the centre of town, and De Gouden Boom (Langestraat 47; ⓦwww.degoudenboom.com), where they've been brewing since 1455. Meanwhile, Het Brugs *Beertje* (Kemelstraat 5) is a small and friendly speciality **beer bar** with a

Chocolate shop, Bruges

stock of three hundred beers, which aficionados reckon is one of the best selections in Belgium.

Chocolate

The major chocolatiers, **Godiva** (Zuidzandstraat 36 ⓦwww.godiva.be) and **Leonidas** (Steenstraat 4 & 82 ⓦwww.leonidas.com), have outlets in Bruges, and their pralines and truffles make a trip to the city worthwhile in itself. But in addition to the big names there are at least fifty smaller stores piled high with the stuff; two to make a beeline for are **Chocolatier Pralinette** (Wollestraat 31b) and **Sukerbuyc** (Katelijnestraat 5). However, chocofiles could start their tour at **Choco-Story** (ⓦwww.choco-story.be), located in the fifteenth-century Maison de Croon. Scholarly types consult the library and explore the pre-Columbian origins of chocolate, while everyone else heads for the lip-smacking demonstration by master chocolatiers and, even better, the degustation.

April in Bruges sees the **Choco-laté Festival** (ⓦwww.choco-late.be), with chocolate artisans showing their wares, from the simple praline to handcrafted chocolate houses.

Porto and the Douro wine route

Gaze across the Douro from the restored riverside promenade in Portugal's second city, **Porto**, and there's no mistaking the dominant industry here. The names of the world's most famous port-wine companies – Croft, Taylor's, Sandeman, Graham's – are spelled out in white letters across the wine-lodge rooftops, while down on the river are tied up a series of handsome *barcos rabelos*, or traditional port-wine boats, formerly used to transport the wine downstream from the Douro's vineyards. A long weekend in the city – easy now Ryanair flies here from London Stansted and Liverpool – gives you plenty of time to explore the revamped city riverfront (now a UNESCO World Heritage Site) but, more to the point, can let you in on the arcane secrets of port-wine making. The wine lodges across the river in the suburb of **Vila Nova de Gaia** all offer tours and tastings, where you'll learn exactly when a wine's good enough to be declared a vintage, and what differentiates a tawny from a ruby. There's no pressure to buy (though there's plenty of opportunity), and all the lodges have English-speaking guides.

We've picked out some of our favourite lodges below, as well as a few great places to taste port in refined surroundings. And while you're in the city, don't miss a river trip on the Douro – plenty of cruises depart daily, from an hour to a full day on the river, with all information and bookings handled by ⓦwww.portotours.com. Otherwise, there's full information about staying in the city on ⓦwww.portoturismo.pt.

Port-wine lodges

Calém ⓦwww.calem.pt. A small Portuguese lodge where they are happy to take just a couple of visitors at a time around the cellars.

Kopke ⓦwww.kopkeports.com. Make a point of visiting the world's oldest port-wine company (founded 1638).

Sandeman ⓦwww.sandeman.com. The highest-profile lodge also has one of the

Porto

slickest tours – there's a good museum here too.
Taylor's ⓦ www.taylor.pt. The real bonus at Taylor's is the first-rate terrace restaurant, the *Barao de Fladgate*, attached to the lodge, which has amazing river views.

Wine and style

Solar do Vinho do Porto Quinta da Macieirinha Porto ⓦ www.ivp.pt. The bar at the Port Wine Institute HQ overlooks the River Douro and is very much the genteel destination for port-wine tasting. Scores are available by the glass, from around €1 and upwards. Closed Sun.
Vinologia Rua de São João 46, Porto ⓦ www.vinologia.eu.com. Bar? Wine shop? Tasting room? No one really can say, but this laid-back French-owned establishment is a great place to start to learn more about Porto's top tipple.
Vintage House Pinhão, ⓦ www.hotelvintagehouse.com. The Douro's most glamorous address is a long way from Porto, near the Spanish border, but you can arrive by boat, train or car and sip wine on your water-facing terrace. The rest of the world seems a long way away here.

Cordon Bleu Paris

In Paris, food is art, top chefs are stars, and dining out is a hallowed pastime, whether it's at the local brasserie or a famed house of *haute cuisine*. So there is no better city for an aspiring cook to learn a few tricks of the trade, either under the wing of the revered **Cordon Bleu** school, or less formally with a **Promenades Gourmandes** cooking class and gourmet walking tour. Your hard-earned skills will certainly help take the stress out of dinner-party preparation once you're back on home turf.

What's more, you're being taught in what is arguably the most captivating city in Europe. Paris may be a metropolis, but it's still a deeply traditional and village-like city, where a leisurely *café au lait* at a pavement café is part of the daily routine. As for the city's **restaurants**, you're in for a real treat. Even the highest of *haute-cuisine* needn't break the bank, and we've listed some of our favourite gastronomic highlights below, for

Alain Ducasse, Paris

all budgets. For true Michelin-starred gastronomy you'll pay something in the region of €100–150 or more per head at dinner, but even in the flashest places a set-price lunch usually costs around half what you'll pay for an evening meal.

Cooking contacts

Le Cordon Bleu Paris Ⓦwww.cordonbleu.edu. The Cordon Bleu, or "Blue Ribbon" was the highest order of chivalry in the Bourbon era, and the term was appropriated in the early nineteenth century when cookery lessons began at the Palais Royal. These days, Cordon Bleu offers a flexible programme of courses, whether you want to spend a few hours learning how to make a good croissant or are studying for a diploma. Students from more than 70 countries study at Le Cordon Bleu, and don't worry if your French isn't up to much – most courses are translated into English. The emphasis is on classic French cuisine, with forays into pastry- and bread-making. From €29 for "Chef's Secrets" demos, €39 for daily demos, €139 for workshops, and €849 for 4-day courses.
Promenandes Gourmandes Ⓦwww.promenadesgourmandes.com. Promenandes Gourmandes aim to give a comprehensive Parisian gourmet experience, from a tour of market as you concoct your menu, through preparation to eating the delicious results. Classes are taught in the Marais kitchen of bilingual cook Paule Caillat, but first Paule will take you on a lively tour of plentiful food markets, as well as the Poilâne bakery and wine shops, so that all the ingredients you source – cheese, bread, meat or spices – will be the finest. From €230 for a half-day class, €330 for a full-day class, and €110 for a walking tour without a class.

Fine restaurants

Alain Ducasse at the Plaza-Athénée Hotel Plaza-Athénée, 25 Av Montaigne, 8e, Ⓦwww.alain-ducasse.com. One of Paris's top *haute cuisine* temples, run by star chef Alain Ducasse, whose sublime dishes, such as Brittany langoustines with Oscietra caviar, are likely to revive even the most jaded palate. The stylish decor features Louis XV-style chairs and Swarowski crystal chandeliers. Around €200 a head.
Ambassade d'Auvergne 22 Rue de Grenier St-Lazare, 3e, Ⓦwww.ambassade-auvergne.com. Suited, mustachioed waiters serve scrumptious Auvergnat cuisine – there's an excellent-value set menu, but you may well be tempted by some of the

house specialities, like the roast guineafowl with garlic.

L'Arpège 84 Rue de Varenne, 7e, ⓦwww.alain-passard.com. Elite chef Alain Passard shocked the gastronomic establishment at his Michelin-starred restaurant by making vegetables the centrepiece of his cuisine. Exhilarating cooking – but budget on €100 as a bare minimum, and book well in advance.

L'Avant Goût 37 Rue Bobillot, 13e. Small neighbourhood restaurant with a big reputation for excitingly good modern French cuisine, and wines to match. The lunch menu is one of the city's best deals.

Perraudin 157 Rue St-Jacques, 5e, ⓦwww.restaurant-perraudin.com. One of the classic bistros of the Left Bank. The atmosphere is thick with Parisian chatter, the menus moderately priced, and the tables brightly lit and tightly packed.

Le Salon d'Hélène 4 Rue d'Assas, 6e. Underneath celebrity chef Hélène Darroze's stratospherically priced gastronomic restaurant, the trendier and more relaxed ground-floor bistro bar offers superbly imaginative tapas-style dishes drawing on her native Basque cuisine.

Le Train Bleu Gare de Lyon, 12e. The sumptuous decor of what must be the world's most luxurious station buffet is straight out of a bygone golden era – everything drips with gilt, and chandeliers hang from high ceilings frescoed with scenes from the Paris-Lyon-Marseilles train route. The traditional French cuisine has a hard time living up to all this, but is still pretty good, if a tad overpriced.

Whisky tasting in Scotland

In Scotland, the national drink is **whisky**, a spirit of far greater subtlety than bland mass-marketed blends might lead you to believe; the best are the single malts, produced by small distilleries from local spring water. Whisky is big business in Scotland, and plenty of producers offer genuinely engaging **tours**, where you can see malted barley being ground into grist, mashed, fermented and distilled into casks. All tours end, of course, with a tempting taster.

There is a great range of **Highland Malts**, with distilleries generously sprinkled through the glens and across the farthest-flung islands. You could take the ferry from John O'Groats or Aberdeen to mesmerizing Orkney, scattered with Neolithic tombs and stone circles, where they've

been distilling Highland Park for more than two hundred years; travel to the wild and mountainous Isle of Skye to sample the peaty west-coast malt Talisker; or head for the less forbidding Isle of Mull, where Tobermory is produced in the pretty harbour town of the same name. The seven-mile **Malt Whisky Trail** (ⓦ www.maltwhiskytrail.com) runs through the fertile Speyside region east of Loch Ness, where you can acquire a taste for Glenlivet, Glenfiddich and Macallan among others. And then there are the distinctive smoky, peaty Islay Malts with enticingly poetic names such as Laguvilin and Laphroaig. They're a good reward for the two-hour ferry trip from Kintyre, and you'll also discover a place relatively untouched by the inroads of tartan tourism. Bladnoch is a **Lowland Malt** distilled near book-loving Wigtown on the Galloway coast, another region off the beaten track of most visitors.

For help **planning your trip**, the best place to start is the website ⓦ www.visit.scotland.com. There's a short list of established whisky-focused tour operators below, as well as a rundown of some of the best distilleries that welcome visitors. For more information on whisky, its history and tasting tips, it's well worth making time to visit the **Scottish Whisky Heritage Centre** in Edinburgh (ⓦ www.whisky-heritage.

co.uk). Plenty of books have been written on the subject too – the most entertaining is the discursive but informative *Raw Spirit: In Search of the Perfect Dram* by Scottish writer and whisky obsessive Iain Banks.

Tour operators

McKinlay Kidd ⓦ www.seescotlanddifferently.co.uk. A wide range of whisky breaks, including the Malt Whisky weekend centred on the Glenmorangie Distillery, where you'll enjoy a tutored tasting, afternoon tea, dinner and a *ceilidh*. They also run a weekend trip to Islay, and a wide-ranging nine-day trip that starts in Edinburgh and takes in Speyside, the Great Glen, Islay and Loch Fyne. Tours from £259.

Scotland Whisky ⓦ www.scotlandwhisky.com. Three-day whisky tour that takes you from a boutique hotel in Edinburgh to a three-course whisky dinner in the Speyside region. In addition to tours of the Edradour, Glenlivet and Glenfiddich distilleries, you'll visit a salmon ladder and the Speyside Cooperage. Tours from £238.

Whisky Tours ⓦ www.whisky-tours.com. A "Winter Warmers" tour takes you to Islay, while the two-week "Where There's an Island" trip includes Islay, Mull, Skye and Orkney. Tours from £567.

Distilleries

Blair Athol ⓦ www.discovering-distilleries.com/blairathol. Located in the Perthshire town of Pitlochry, Blair Athol is one of Scotland's oldest distilleries, founded in 1798. Their product is a mellow, twelve-year-old single malt.

Glengoyne ⓦ www.glengoyne.com. Situated near the banks of Loch Lomond, this distillery welcomes visitors with open arms – there are a range of options from the basic tour plus dram to high-powered masterclasses.

Glenkinchie ⓦ www.discovering-distilleries.com/glenkinchie. The water that goes to blend this whisky runs from the Lammermuir hills near Edinburgh and has a hint of chalk, which they claim modifies the Lowland malt taste.

Glenlivet ⓦ www.theglenlivet.com. The best known of the Speyside malts; it's a highly professional operation with engaging tours.

Highland Park ⓦ www.highlandpark. Regular tours allow you to explore the history of this rich and complex Orkney single malt, which operated illegally in its early years in the late eighteenth century.

Laphroaig ⓦ www.laphroaig.com. Peaty, pungent Islay malts divide the critics, but you're sure to enjoy both a trip to the island itself, and the entertaining distillery tours.

Tapas in Madrid

There's no better place in Europe than the Spanish capital, **Madrid**, to get to grips with **tapas** – those little dishes of food that have taken the world by storm. And it's not just about eating, but is rather a whole way of life for the inhabitants, the *madrileños*, who seem to spend much of their time ensconced in a café or bar, eating, drinking, gossiping and arguing. Starting at noon, and then again from around 8pm, the city's tapas bars fill with customers, who move from one place to another to sample the house specialities, from crisply fried squid to sliced cheese, cured anchovies to *patatas bravas* (spicy potatoes). And remember – for the locals, this is just a warm-up for lunch and dinner. Of course, you can happily fill up instead at the bar of your choice, in which case it's best to be in a group so that you can mix and match dishes.

Bars and cafés known as *tabernas*, *tascas*, *bodegas* or *cervecerías* are all places that serve tapas (sometimes also called *pinchos*). Basically, you'll get mini-portions of meat, fish, tortilla or salad for €1.50–3 a plate – the larger portions of tapas, known as *raciones* (€5–10), make a sufficient meal in themselves. Madrid's narrow, atmospheric alleys and wide, open boulevards are filled with possibilities – we list some of our favourites below – but you can't go wrong if you follow the crowds, and watch what the locals are ordering. Local listings services like ⓦwww.guidelocio.com, ⓦwww.in-madrid.com and ⓦwww.gomadrid.com can offer more ideas too.

The best tapas bars

Cervecería Santa Ana Plaza de Santa Ana 10. Excellent spot for alfresco or indoor tapas and beers.

El Abuelo c/Victoria 12. This legendary family-owned tapas bar serves only two tapas: grilled prawns and prawns cooked with garlic.

La Musa de Latina Costanilla de San Andres 12. Brings Spanish cooking to the next level with a new way of making tapas.

La Venencia c/Echegaray 7. Marvellous old wooden bar, serving sherry only and the

most basic of tapas – cheese and pressed tuna. An absolute must.
Los Gabrieles c/Echegaray 17. One of the most spectacular tiled bars in Madrid, with fabulous nineteenth-century drinking scenes on the ceramic tiles, including a great version of Velázquez's *Los Borrachos* (The Drunkards).
Taberna de Antonio Sànchez c/Mesón de Parades 13. Quality tapas served up at this 100-year-old bar.
Taberna de Cienvinos c/Nuncio 17. Wonderfully atmospheric old *taberna* serving a huge variety of wines plus tapas and *raciones*.
Taberna Maceira c/Huertas 66. Tasty tapas and seafood; *pulpo a la Gallega* (octopus with red paprika) is one of its specialities.

Outdoors and nature

Outdoors and nature

Sleigh-riding in Transylvania
The Leiden tulip fields
Walking in the English Lake District
Cycling in France
Climbing the Swiss Alps
Sailing in Greece

Sleigh-riding in Transylvania

Thanks to Bram Stoker's novel, rugged Transylvania in central and western Romania is famed abroad as the homeland of Count Dracula, but you'll find there's a lot more to explore here than the story of a bloodthirsty nobleman. Steeped in history and legend, it offers some of the most beautiful but least-known scenery in Europe. Deeply rural Transylvania abounds with soaring mountains, impressive caves, alpine meadows, dense forests, and lowland valleys with quaint villages and buffalo cooling off in the rivers. There are rich opportunities for exploration well off the beaten track, from high-roofed wooden churches to some pretty wild wildlife – bears and wolves still roam here.

The population is a mix of Romanians, Magyars, Germans, Gypsies and others, thanks to centuries of migration and colonization. Holidays in Transylvania can connect you with these ancient cultures and their rich traditions; indeed, a wonderfully romantic way of discovering this landscape in winter is to traverse it by **horse-drawn sleigh**. A number of tour operators run all-inclusive trips that take care of the practicalities and ensure that you enjoy a smooth ride. Depending on your level of fitness and experience, you can either drive the sleigh yourself, or sit back, wrap up warm and let someone else do the hard work.

Tour operators

Responsible Travel ⓦ www.responsibletravel.com. This is a good option for ethical travellers: Responsible Travel provides year-round employment for local people, and the majority of the supplies come from nearby farmers and craftspeople. The winter breaks in February allow you to explore the snow-covered mountains by sleigh or in the saddle. 7 days from £645.

Riding Holidays in Transylvania ⓦ www.riding-holidays.ro. A week-long itinerary based in Lunca Ilvei village, with (optional) riding to see spectacular mountain views plus sleigh rides in the forest, where you might see the tracks left by wolves, bears and lynx. There's also a market visit.

Transylvania Uncovered ⓦ www.beyondtheforest.com. You stay in the traditional Transylvanian village of Miclosoara and take part in activities from bird-watching to hiking, as well as sleigh rides in winter. From £769.

The Leiden tulip fields

Spring is the perfect time to visit the Netherlands, to see the spectacular tulip fields. They are a glorious sight, complemented by a stay in the delightful little town of **Leiden**, whose charm lies principally in the peace and prettiness of its gabled streets and canals. Its most appealing quarter is a pedestrianized area that is home to the country's principal archeological museum, while Breestraat marks the site of a vigorous market (Wed and Sat), which sprawls right over the sequence of bridges into Haarlemmerstraat, the town's major shopping street.

The view from the train between Leiden and Haarlem provides terrific views of the **tulips**, as the line cuts directly through the main growing areas, the bulbfields divided into stark geometric blocks of pure colour. Should you want to get closer, make a bee-line for the **Keukenhof Gardens** (open daily from the end of March to mid-May; ⓦwww.keukenhof.nl), the largest flower gardens in the world. Some six million blooms are on show for their full flowering period, complemented by 5000 square metres of greenhouses. Special buses run daily on a regular service to the Keukenhof from Leiden bus station. It's also worth knowing that between April and September many towns in this area of the Netherlands have a flower parade featuring decorated floats, floral displays and processions.

Frequent **trains** connect Leiden with Amsterdam – it's a 45-minute ride, and full timetables (and ticket sales) are available on ⓦwww.ns.nl, the Netherlands Railways website. Local **accommodation** includes the cosy, canalside *Nieuw Minerva* hotel (ⓦwww.nieuwminerva.nl), though there are plenty more hotels viewable on ⓦwww.bookings.nl.

Walking in the English Lake District

The glacier-carved **Lake District National Park** in Cumbria is England's most popular walking area, home to the country's highest mountains, deepest lakes and, arguably, most sensational scenery. It's almost alpine in character, albeit with a definite English twist – think stone-built villages, ivy-clad country pubs and somnolent village greens – and you certainly don't need to be a gung-ho hiker to appreciate its matchless mountains (known hereabouts as fells), waterfalls and lakes. Whatever your level of fitness or expertise, you can find a Lake District walk to suit – from an hour's stroll up to a local viewpoint to an all-day circuit around various peaks and valleys. Moreover, you're never very far from a rest-stop, with flagstoned hikers' bars, enticing teashops and sturdy country hotels at every turn, where they won't turn up their noses at the sight of muddy boots.

The Lake District, England

Weather in the Lakes

The weather in Cumbria changes quickly, but the sudden shifts of light on the bracken and moorland grasses, and on the slate of the local buildings, are part of the area's appeal. Keep in touch with the vagaries of the weather with **www.lakedistrict.gov.uk/weatherline**, a one-day advance forecast for the fells and valleys, including hiking conditions. It goes without saying that at all times of the year you need to be equipped with warm waterproof gear and a decent pair of walking boots.

If you're not confident about being able to find your own way, or simply want someone else to do the organizing, then it's probably best to join a guided tour (see listings below). The **Lake District National Park Authority** (www.lake-district.gov.uk) also organizes guided walks throughout the year – details available on the website or posted at local tourist offices – while their "Miles Without Stiles" programme suggests low-level routes that are accessible to all abilities. The tourist authority for the region, **Cumbria Tourism** (www.golakes.co.uk), meanwhile, has many more suggestions and can fill you in on accommodation and other services. And you might well want to call on the services of **Sherpa Van** (www.sherpavan.com), a daily door-to-door baggage service for walkers and cyclists between overnight stops on the Coast-to-Coast, Sea-to-Sea, Cumbria Way and Dales Way.

Specialist walking-tour operators

Contours Walking Holidays www.contours.co.uk. Large variety of self-guided walking holidays along the Cumbria Way, Dales Way and Coast-to-Coast, starting at £210 for four nights' B&B, walking 10–12 miles a day.
Discovery Travel www.discoverytravel.co.uk. Self-guided walking tours, following the Cumbria Way or a Lakeland Round circuit, though a single-centre Keswick walking holiday (from £325) is also available. Prices include B&B accommodation, maps and guides, baggage transfer and emergency support.
Knobbly Stick www.knobblystick.com. "The easy way to take a walk on the wild

side" – fully guided four- to seven-night (three to six days' walking) holidays, based in comfortable hotels at Ullswater, Keswick, Wasdale, Grasmere and the southern Lakes, from £385, including dinner, bed and breakfast, guiding and transport.
Walking Women ⓦ www.walkingwomen.com. Women-only guided walking trips to suit all abilities in Borrowdale, Grasmere, Derwent Water and the western Lakes. Two- to four-night tours, from £150, on a B&B or full-board basis.

Cycling in France

The home of the Tour de France enjoys a deep love affair with the bicycle, making it an ideal country to explore on two wheels, whether you opt for exploring the coastal paths and ancient settlements of Brittany, the vineyards and fairytale châteaux of the Loire, or the lavender-rich fields of Provence. And of course one of the joys of France is that you're pretty much guaranteed a delicious meal and a good glass of wine at the end of each day.

A growing number of **cycling tour operators** will help organize your cycling trip, tailoring routes to your fitness level, supplying bikes to your specifications, booking characterful accommodation and transporting your bags, leaving you free to pedal from village to village. Most tours involve cycling from 10 miles per day up to 40 miles on the more strenuous routes. Be sure to check your capabilities at home before you book a break, and study your chosen route carefully, bearing in mind that gradient can be a bigger factor than mileage.

French villages are well accustomed to cyclists parading round in garish gear, and all larger towns have at least one hire agency. **Bike rental** is also available at many hotels, campsites, tourist offices, train stations and even restaurants along the way. If you are used to your own bike, and can't imagine riding anything else, all is not lost. Eurostar (ⓦ www.eurostar.com) will **transport your bike** for free if you remove the wheels and put it in a bike bag. On the speedy TGV services within France you will also have to have a bike bag, but the regional TER trains let you put your bike in the luggage van or in the compartment. *Cycle Touring in France* by Stephen

On your bike in the Loire valley

Thanks to the **Loire à Vélo** scheme (ⓦwww.loire-a-velo.fr), a mix of dedicated cycle paths and meticulously signposted routes along minor roads now runs almost all the way along the Loire from Orléans to beyond Angers – a distance of more than 300km. The region around Blois offers an additional, 300-kilometre network, **Châteaux à Vélo** (ⓦwww.chateauxavelo.com). Meanwhile, the **Detours de Loire** scheme (ⓦwww.locationdevelos.com) allows you to pick up a bike in one place and drop it off in another, paying inexpensive drop-off costs per zone crossed.

Fox, published by Cicerone, is a must if you're planning your own itinerary without the help of a tour operator.

Cycling tour operators

Belle France ⓦwww.bellefrance.co.uk. Mainly circular routes in northern France, with all the practicalities expertly catered for. Trips are self-guided, so you go at your own pace. The Loire Discovery trip, graded "easy", costs from £700 for 7 nights.

Cycling for Softies ⓦwww.cycling-for-softies.co.uk. As the name suggests, these are easy routes, with enjoyable itineraries scattered throughout France. They suggest the Mayenne and Sarte route as a perfect introduction to the experience as much of the cycling is along towpaths. From £378 for 3 nights.

French Cycling Holidays ⓦwww.frenchcyclingholidays.com. Well-organized guided tours in the Loire, Burgandy, Dordogne, Bordeaux, Languedoc and Provence. The Languedoc trip takes advantage of the scenic towpaths along the Canal du Midi; from £965 for 6 nights.

Headwater ⓦwww.headwater.com. Varied itineraries, from the vineyards, cherry orchards and Gothic cathedrals of Alsace to the stunning valleys of the Dordogne and the *bastide* towns of the Lot. From £600 per week.

Climbing the Swiss Alps

Don't worry – we don't mean you're going to be doing the climbing, rather taking the rack-railways and cable cars that link Swiss mountain villages to even the highest Alpine peaks. The spectacular **Jungfrau** region in the Bernese Oberland is named after a grand triple-peaked ridge (the Eiger, Mönch and Jungfrau) which crests at 4000m, but even here you can be whisked to the summits without lifting a finger.

The rack-railway excursion up to the **Jungfraujoch** (®www.jungfrau.com) coils spectacularly across mountain pastures before breaking through the treeline and tunnelling clean through the Eiger to emerge at the highest railway station in Europe (3454m). It's a bit of a circus, and overflowing with tour groups, but nonetheless on a clear day the heart-thumping views – across to Germany's Black Forest one way, Italian Alps the other – are very definitely worth it. Footpaths linking all the stations en route mean that you can see and do a great deal in a day and still get back to **Interlaken** (the main town and departure point) or even Bern or Zürich by bedtime. The cable-car ride up the **Schilthorn** (2970m) gets second billing, but is in fact quicker, cheaper, offers an even more scenic ride up and has better views. You'll have seen the cable car put to dramatic effect in 007's *On Her Majesty's Secret Service*. What's more, you get to sip cocktails at the top in the revolving summit restaurant. The Schilthorn

Winter warmers

If you're in Switzerland in the winter months, you'll find that nothing warms you up like the hearty national cuisine. Cheese **fondue** – a pot of wine-laced molten cheese into which you dip cubes of bread or potato – is the signature Swiss dish, and is most fun shared. Another speciality is **raclette** – piquant molten cheese spread on a plate and scooped up with bread or potato. A Swiss-German staple is **rösti**, grated potatoes fried to a golden-brown hash and topped with cheese, chopped ham or a fried egg. All delicious, though none of it easy on the waistline.

cablecar (@www.schilthorn.ch) is accessed from the **Lauterbrunnen** valley, itself probably the most beautiful part of the whole region – the **Staubbach Falls**, the highest in Switzerland (300mm), tumble just beyond Lauterbrunnen village, while there's also a funicular from the village up to car-free **Mürren** for more dazzling views.

Nearest airport to the region is Bern, 60km away, though easyJet flies into Basel-Mulhouse, which is still only two hours by direct train from Interlaken. Other European airlines use Zürich, again only a couple of hours away by train. For local information, including details of accommodation, excursions and events, consult the useful @www.interlaken.ch.

Sailing in Greece

Nothing liberates you from day-to-day stress like **sailing in Greece**: standing at the helm of a yacht in the sunshine, diving from the side into sparkling blue seas, and choosing which tranquil little bay you're going to dock at for the night. If you're a novice, Greece is the perfect place to learn to sail – the weather is kind and the water generally deep and tranquil, so you won't have to contend with complex tide tables, shallows or sand banks. What's more, with 166 inhabited islands, Greece offers a whole host of wonderful sailing possibilities.

The **Cyclades** is the most satisfying Greek archipelago for island-hopping, with its vibrant capital on Sýros. The majority of the islands are arid and rocky, with brilliant-white, cubist architecture. Arriving by boat at the partially submerged volcanic cone of Santoríni is one of the world's great travel adventures, while one major ancient site worth making time for is Delos, the commercial and religious centre of the classical Greek world.

Further east still, the **Dodecanese** islands lie so close to the Turkish coast that some are almost within hailing distance of the shore. Medieval Rhodes is the most famous, but almost every one has its classical remains, its Crusaders' castle, its traditional villages and grandiose, Italian-built Art Deco public buildings.

In the **northeastern Aegean**, Híos is culturally fascinating, while Lésvos is more of an acquired taste, though once smitten you may find it hard to leave. The six **Ionian islands** are, both geographically and culturally, a mixture of Greece and Italy. Floating on the haze of the Adriatic, their green silhouettes come as a surprise to those more used to the stark outlines of the Aegean. The most famous is Corfu, but for a less touristy experience, head for Kefalloniá or Itháki. **Crete** meanwhile is distinguished as the home of the Minoan civilization, Europe's earliest, which made the island the centre of a maritime trading empire as early as 2000 BC and produced artworks unsurpassed in the ancient world.

Sailing schools

Aegean Sailing School ⓦ www.aegeansailingschool.com. They run the "Competent Crew" course for complete beginners, offering all the support you'll need, while "Day Skipper" gives you the skills to sail independently. You'll be sailing in the beautiful Saronic and Argolic Gulfs. 5-day courses from €850.

Concept Holidays ⓦ www.conceptholidays.co.uk. These courses are run from Askeli Bay in Poros, a picturesque little island just an hour from Athens. Royal Yacht Association-qualified trainers teach sailing along with windsurfing and kayaking. 5-day courses from £599.

Odyssey Sailing ⓦ www.odysseysailing.gr. Five-day courses held in Skiathos; you sail to nearby islands and bays, with instruction geared to your level of experience. From €920.

Sail Ionian ⓦ www.sailionian.co.uk. A friendly family-run company based on the island of Levkas in the South Ionian Sea. They offer "assisted sailing" for inexperienced or nervous sailors, as well as more advanced courses. Training instructor per day €200.

Pampering

Pampering

The Blue Lagoon, Iceland
Bohemian spa towns
A Turkish bath in İstanbul
Retreats in the UK
European boutique hotels

The Blue Lagoon, Iceland

There are few more surreal outdoor experiences in Europe than a wallow in the soothing waters of Iceland's famous **Blue Lagoon** (Ⓦwww.bluelagoon.com). Surprisingly perhaps, for a land full of geysers, it's not a natural phenomenon – a nearby power plant pumps geothermally heated water from a mile under the surface and uses it to supply Icelandic homes, while the (safe and clean!) run-off fills the lagoon. The water is of Blue Flag quality and, ringed by black basalt and the futuristic chimneys of the power station, the lagoon certainly provides one of the region's more memorable experiences. Not surprisingly, it often turns up as the backdrop to photo-shoots and music videos.

Many people tag on a visit here to the beginning or end of an Iceland mini break, as the lagoon is only 20 minutes from the airport or 45 min-

The Blue Lagoon, Iceland

utes from downtown Reykjavik. Even in summer in Iceland the outdoor temperature is unlikely to top 20°C, so with the Blue Lagoon's water at around 37–39°C, and coloured a very startling shade of milky blue, no one is in any hurry to leave, particularly as it abounds with minerals said to have curative properties – the Icelanders themselves swear by a dip, while an energizing waterfall, lava cave, steam bath and sauna add up to a full spa experience. Facilities here are excellent, and with a good restaurant also on site, it's easy to spend most of the day pampering yourself.

Reykjavik is served by Icelandair and Iceland Express, while many tour operators include a visit to the Blue Lagoon as part of their programmes. For more ideas on holidays in Iceland, from glacier hiking to exploring Reykjavik, see Ⓦwww.icelandvisitor.com, Ⓦwww.icelandtotal.com and Ⓦwww.tour.is, while the **Iceland Tourist Board** (Ⓦwww.icelandtouristboard.com) can help with the practical side of your visit.

Bohemian spa towns

West of the Czech capital, Prague, towards the German border, Bohemia's famous **spa region** enjoys a sparkling reputation. Taking the waters is an age-old means of shedding aches and pains, and the allure of "the cure" is still very much intact. The spa tradition dates back to Roman times and, while its curative properties may not be scientifically proven, it is certainly a shortcut to some serious relaxation and battery-charging. Indeed, with Prague now firmly on the European city-break circuit – and already too oversubscribed for some – the largely unsung Bohemian spa towns could be just what the doctor ordered.

There are regular flights to Prague with easyJet, among others, and from there you can take the train to the spa region – 3 daily services run to Karlovy Vary (journey time 4–5hr) and up to 10 to Mariánské Lázně (3hr). See Ⓦwww.czech.cz for help planning your trip and go to Ⓦwww.spas.cz and Ⓦwww.czechspavacations.com for specialized information on the country's spa resorts.

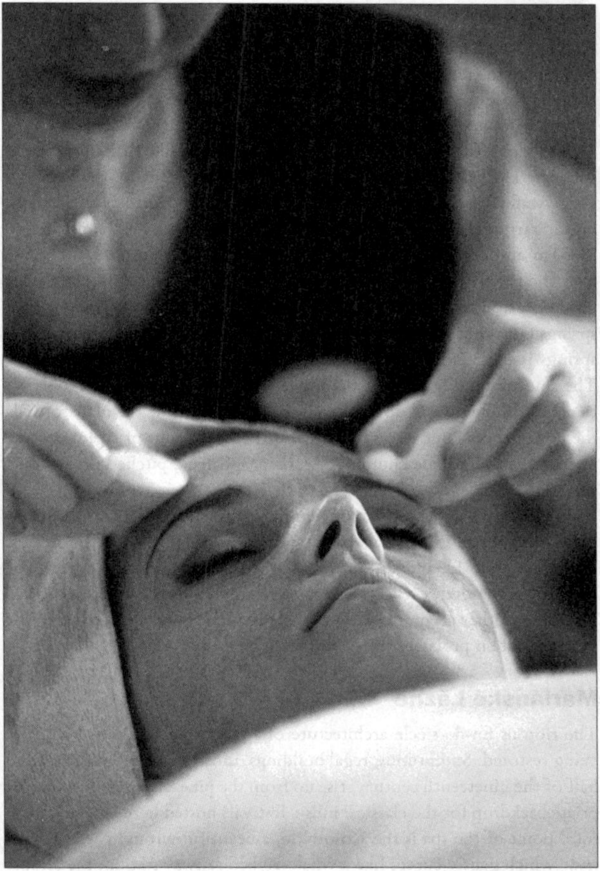

Karlovy Vary

Karlovy Vary, undisputed king of the Bohemian spas, is one of the most cosmopolitan Czech towns. Its international clientele – largely Russians – annually doubles the local population. The best way to take in Karlovy Vary is to wander up the river stopping to sip the medicinal water at the springs along the way. You can buy kitsch teapot-like drinking cups at souvenir kiosks. The water is hot and surprisingly salty – the delicious sweet wafers you'll see people munching are designed to take away the taste. Start at the **Thermal**, a fairly brutal Communist-era construction that has an open-air, spring-water swimming pool with fantastic views over the town. As the valley narrows, the river disappears under a wide terrace in front of the graceful **Mlyýnská kolonáda**, each of whose four springs is more scalding than the last. Most powerful of the town's twelve springs is the **Vřídlo**, which belches out over 2500 gallons every hour. The smooth marble floor of the modern **Vřídelní kolonáda** allows patients to shuffle up and down contentedly, while inside the glass rotunda the geyser shoots hot water forty feet upwards. Clouds of steam obscure a view of the Baroque church of Maria Magdaléna, pitched nearby on a precipitous site.

On Karlovy Vary's most famous shopping street, the Stará louka, stands the **Grand Hotel Pupp** (Ⓦ www.pupp.cz) founded in 1701 as the greatest hotel in the world, and still maintaining a certain snooty grandeur. The local town website, Ⓦ www.karlovyvary.cz, has plenty of information in English on other accommodation, plus restaurants and spa facilities. The swishest **café** is probably the *Elefant* on Stará louka.

Mariánské Lázně

The riotous fin-de-siècle architecture of **Mariánské Lázně** is gradually being restored. Sumptuous, regal buildings, most dating from the second half of the nineteenth century, rise up from the pine-clad hills – an appropriate backdrop for the classical music festivals hosted here annually. The focal point of the spa is the **Kolonáda**, a beautiful wrought-iron colonnade which gently curves like a whale-ribbed railway station, the atmosphere relentlessly genteel and sober. The spa's first and foremost spring, known as Křížový pramen, has its own adjoining Neoclassical colonnade. Mariánské Lázně's altitude lends an almost sub-alpine freshness to the air, and walking is as important to "the cure" as the various specialized treatments; maps showing marked walks in the area are available in hotels and shops. *Café Polonia* is probably Mariánské Lázně's most opulent **café**, offering stucco decoration as rich as its cakes.

A Turkish bath in İstanbul

Arriving in **İstanbul** – a city poised between East and West - can come as a bit of a shock. The former imperial capital is a heady mix of the European and Oriental and in the old city, in and around the Sultanahmet district, the back streets teem with traders pushing handcarts, stevedores carrying burdens twice their size, and omnipresent shoeshine boys. Men still monopolize the public bars and teahouses, while many women cover their heads. It may not seem like the ideal place for a chilled-out break, but this is merely one aspect of modern İstanbul: the city has one of the youngest populations in Europe and in recent years a host of pavement cafés and elegant bars has sprung up. And as well as some of the most absorbing historic sights in the world, from the mighty dome of Aya Sofya to the Ottoman Topkapı Palace, the city presents one unique relaxation experience – the Turkish bath or *hamam*.

The culture of the *hamam* grew out of Muslim cleansing rituals, and became associated with significant occasions and rites of passage. In a culture where women's lives were strictly delineated, the *hamam* was also a place where a degree of social liberation, interaction and even gossip was possible. Many of the baths in the city were built in the Ottoman era, and are places of great peace and beauty, decorated with geometric tiles and with shafts of light penetrating their high domed roofs. Traditionally there was a good deal of paraphernalia associated with a visit to the *hamam*: women would take an array of silken drying cloths, as well as wooden clogs (per-

The covered bazaar

İstanbul's Kapalı Çarşı, or **Covered Bazaar** (Mon–Sat 8.30am–6.30 or 7.30pm), is a huge web of passageways housing over 4000 shops. It has long since spilled out of the covered area, sprawling into the surroundings streets. As well as items associated with the *hamam*, there are carpet shops everywhere catering for all budgets, plus stores selling leather goods around Kurkçular Kapı and Perdahçılar Caddesi, and gold jewellery on Kuyumcular Caddesi. You'll need to be prepared to haggle, and when you need a break the *Fes Café* on Halıcilar Caddesi is a comfortable spot to gloat over your purchases.

haps inlaid with mother-of-pearl), a copper soap case and a mitt to slough off dead skin. A jewellery box was used to store treasures for the duration of the bath, and mirrors, henna bowls and perfume were essential for beautification purposes. Although these items aren't really part of the modern *hamam* experience, all are available in the Covered Bazaar (see box) and they make great souvenirs.

The baths are still strictly **segregated** – having undressed in the outer room or *camekan*, you enter the steamy heart of the *hamam*. On a raised heated platform in the centre you'll receive a wonderfully vigorous massage, and have your dead skin scrubbed away. Most people take advantage of the reclining couches in the changing cubicles to recover – you may find that the instant detox leaves you feeling a little light-headed.

The *hamam* in the centre of İstanbul are those most frequented by tourists – see the listings below for details. However, it's worth knowing that outside the main tourist areas *hamams* are much cheaper. Even so, prices are low by Western European standards.

Hamams

Çemberlitaş Hamam Divan Yolu, Sultanahmet. Dimly lit and very beautiful 400-year-old baths near the Covered Bazaar, open daily from 6am to midnight – as with all baths, there are separate posted hours for men and women. Around €15.

Cağaoğlu Hamam Hilali Ahmed Caddesi 34, Cağaoğlu. You're guaranteed a vigorous massage at this ancient hamam, which is said to have hosted the bizarre triumvirate of Franz Liszt, Florence Nightingale and Tony Curtis. Women's sessions here run daily from 8am to 8pm. Prices range €10–30.
Tophane Hamam On the Bosphorus at Tophane. These 500-year-old baths lie out of the centre, but sessions here (daily 7am–10pm) cost only around €4.

Retreats in the UK

An increasingly popular antidote to daily stress is to go on a **retreat**, the ultimate get-away-from-it-all option. Retreats take many forms – you might want to expand your mind with some meditation, or stretch your muscles with some yoga. There's nothing like a luxury spa to give you an all-round sense of well-being, while some retreats simply offer peaceful accommodation in a rural location where you can find space and time to think. We've picked out three examples below of retreat options in England, Scotland and Wales, but contact the **Retreat Company** (Ⓦwww.theretreatcompany.com) for further ideas.

Retreat centres

Pen Rhiw Ⓦwww.penrhiw.co.uk. A secluded house on the St David's Peninsula in Wales, offering home-cooked veggie food, optional yoga and meditation, massage and guided walks. Log fires make this a snug winter hideaway. Accommodation from £19 per person.
TOR Spa Retreat Ⓦwww.torsparetreat.com. This spa centre at Ickham, Canterbury in Kent, is founded on the principles of Ayurveda, an Indian philosophy of harmonizing mind and body through diet and massage. There's a Finnish sauna and a hydro pool, and plenty of space to relax and unwind. With only twelve spa guests at any one time, you have a very personal welcome. From £70 per day.
Yogoloji Ⓦwww.yogoloji.com. Stay in a Highland wilderness retreat, with therapy rooms, gym, sauna and yoga hall. The chef whips up healthy locally sourced food, and in addition to the usual retreat activities you can cycle, fly-fish and feed the estate deer. 4-night stay £1400, 5-night stay £1750, 9-night stay £2800.

European boutique hotels

Whether you're in the heart of a city or out in the wilds, accommodation is central to your travel experience. Europe boasts some stunning **boutique hotels**: small, intimate establishments where a warm welcome, personal service and individual decor are the key to a relaxing and memorable stay. We've picked out some of our favourites below; check out the boutique hotel directory Ⓦ www.mrandmrssmith.com for further ideas.

Stay in style

Artus Hotel, Paris Ⓦ www.artushotel.com. A hip and happening hotel in stylish St Germaine, with unique artworks in every room – each of the guest room doors, for example, was individually designed by a different artist. Jacuzzis and luxury bathrooms ensure a truly decadent stay. From €235.

Choupana Hills, Madeira Ⓦ www.choupanahills.com. This understated hotel overlooking the Madeiran capital, Funchal, blends beautifully with its subtropical surroundings – the spa facilities ensure days of blissful relaxation and the restaurant, with produce sourced from Funchal's excellent market, is superbly inventive. From €247.

Hazlitt's, London Ⓦ www.hazlitts.co.uk. Hazlitt's proves that you can get away from it all in central London – this swish Soho hideaway is housed in a 300 year old building and pays great attention to period detail, with clawfoot baths and ornate oak beds. From £175.

Hotel Cortiina, Munich Ⓦ www.cortiina.com. This is a calming city-centre option with impeccable design: features include parquet flooring, oak panelling and minimalist stone fireplaces. Staff will book theatre, opera and restaurants for you, or just stay indoors at the chic cocktail bar. From €156.

Il Palazetto, Rome Ⓦ www.palazettoroma.com. A simply unbeatable location overlooking the Spanish Steps. Connected to the Wine Academy of Rome and decked out in classic style and in soothingly pale hues, it effortlessly combines old-world charm and thoroughly modern luxuries. From €210.

Son Brull, Mallorca Ⓦ www.sonbrull.com. A restful twelfth-century monastery, converted with confident simplicity. There's a spa and indoor and outdoor pools; tennis, yachting and bike rental can be arranged if you're feeling more energetic. From €248.

Boutique Hotel bedroom

Shopping

Shopping

Hitting the sales in Milan
The souk in Marrakesh
Flea markets in Paris
Interior design in Copenhagen
Fashion and antiques in Brussels

Hitting the sales in Milan

Milan is synonymous with shopping: whether you're here to indulge in the ultimate consumer experience or want to bag a designer bargain, there are few places on earth with more to offer. The annual sales start in the second week of January, and you need to make a beeline for the so-called Quadrilatero d'Oro, or "Golden Rectangle", home to all the big fashion names, along with design studios and contemporary art galleries. Everything is concentrated in less than a square mile, so you won't have far to walk, but many of the stores have fancy cafés for when you need to take the pressure off your Manolos – like the oh-so-stylish *Bar Martini* at Dolce & Gabbana Womenswear (Corso Venezia 15). Others feature spas, hairdressers and even gyms, while at the uber-chic Trussardi Women (Piazza della Scala 5) there's a contemporary art gallery.

For designer labels at affordable prices, you could always rummage through the many **factory outlets** around town, or check out the city's wide range of medium- and budget-range clothes shops. Milan also excels in **furniture and design**, with showrooms from the world's top companies, plus a handful of shops offering a selection of brands and labels under one roof.

Most shops open from Tuesday to Saturday 10am to 12.30pm and 3.30 to 7pm, plus Monday afternoons, although some larger places also stay open

Where to shop till you drop

For **designer fashion**, the Quadrilatero d'Oro (Via Montenapoleone, Via della Spiga and around) houses Versace, Prada et al, while Corso di Porta Ticinese has a mix of funkier, independent shops, as well as international names like Diesel, Carhartt and Stussy. Corso Vittorio Emanuele, Via Torino and Corso Buenos Aires sport Italian mid-range chain stores and international **high-street** giants alike. Corso Europa, Via Durini, Corso Venezia and Corso Monforte are home to the **furniture and lighting** showrooms that made Milan the design capital of the world in the 1950s.

at lunchtime and on Sunday afternoons. There are daily flights from the UK to Milan from London airports, Glasgow, Liverpool and Newcastle with easyJet, Ryanair, Flybe and others; go to ⓦwww.milanoinfotourist.com for help with trip practicalities.

Fashion stores

Gianfranco Ferré Via Sant'Andrea 15 ⓦwww.gianfranco ferre.com. Ferré's new boutique has a stunning red resin wall, but it is the adjoining day-spa that makes it really special.

Giorgio Armani Via Manzoni 31 ⓦwww.armani.com. This temple to all things Giorgio is more a mini-shopping centre than a shop. There are boutiques for all his ranges – women and menswear, furnishings and houseware – plus the relaxed *Armani Café* and a pricey Japanese restaurant, *Nobu* (with fantastically offhand service). With a book corner, in-house florists and chocolate counter you really won't need to go anywhere else.

Gucci Via Montenapoleone 5–7, & Galleria Vittorio Emanuele II ⓦwww.gucci.com. Every desirable fashion item imaginable is available in the warren of sleek show-

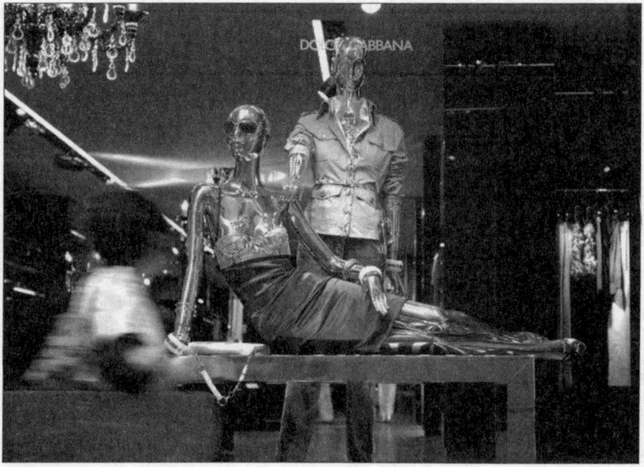

rooms in Via Montenapoleone, while the newer store in the Galleria Vittorio Emanuele II has the elegant, minimalist *Gucci* café.

Just Cavalli Boutique Via della Spiga 30 ⓦ www.robertocavalli.net. Cavalli's leopard-skin-clad clientele feels wonderfully at home in the white-cloud lift or shimmering up and down the giant central staircase. The pièce de résistance, however, is the café, *Just Cavalli Food*, where an aquarium swims with brightly coloured fish.

Prada Galleria Vittorio Emanuele II ⓦ www.prada.com. The original Prada store, dating from 1913, stands on a side corner in the centre of the Galleria Vittorio Emanuele II. Much of the elegant interior is original, but the best bit is the central staircase swirling down past the leather goods to the men's and women's collections in the basement.

Factory outlets

DT Intrend Galleria San Carlo 6, near the Duomo. Offering discounts on the Max Mara brands.

Il Salvagente Via Bronzetti 16 ⓦ www.salvagentemilano.it. The grande dame of Milan's outlet stores, where, with a little rummaging, you can bag a designer label for around a third of its original price.

Design and furniture

B&B Italia Via Durini 14 ⓦ www.bebitalia.it. Specializes in stylish contemporary furniture with collections by the big names in Italian modern design.

Cassina Via Durini 16 ⓦ www.cassina.it. The showroom of this legendary Milanese company is always worth a visit for both new designs and their range of twentieth-century design classics, including Eames, De Stijl and Rennie Mackintosh chairs.

De Padova Corso Venezia 14 ⓦ www.depadova.it. Two floors of elegant own-brand designer furniture and houseware artfully displayed in a stylish showroom.

Driade Via Manzoni 30 ⓦ www.driade.com. A wonderful multi-brand store with their own designs, as well as work by designers like Ron Arad and Philippe Starck. There's furniture, tableware, kitchen and bathroom accessories, but the real treat here is the showroom housed in an elegant nineteenth-century palazzo.

High Tech Pizza XXV Aprile 12 ⓦ www.high-techmilano.com. Great for getting lost among designer, imitation and ethnic knick-knacks.

Speciality food shops

Peck Via Spadari 7–9. Three floors of Italian delicacies, from olive oil and home-made chocolate to mouth-watering cheeses and an impressive wine cellar. There's also a café on the first floor and a swish cocktail bar and restaurant round the corner at Via Cantù 3.

Cova Via Montenapoleone 8. Banks of irresistible cakes and confectionery are on offer at this famous tearoom dating back to the Napoleonic era.

Il Salumaio Via Montenapoleone 12 ⓦwww.ilsalumaiodimontenapoleone.it. The selection of savoury delicacies and handmade pasta are to die for in this smart delicatessen, with a café and tables outside in the courtyard.

The souk in Marrakesh

The central Moroccan city of **Marrakesh** is a city of immense beauty, sitting low, pink and tent-like before a great shaft of mountains. It might seem like a long way to go to the shops, but – trust us – you've never seen markets quite like this. It's also a perfect destination for a winter break; even in the coolest months the climate is a delight. City-break operators are starting to pick up on Marrakesh's attractions, and British Airways flies here from London Gatwick, as does Atlas Blue, North Africa's low-cost airline. For much more information about Morocco in general, visit the Moroccan tourist board's website (ⓦwww.tourisme-marocain.com) as well as useful sites like ⓦwww.morocco.com and ⓦwww.arab.net/morocco.

Shopping, Moroccan style

Marrakesh's vast central square, the **Djemaa el Fna**, is the stage for a long-established ritual in which shifting circles of onlookers gather around groups of acrobats, drummers, pipe musicians, dancers, storytellers and comedians, while the experience of shopping in the neighbouring **souk** is second to none. Providing you have a sense of humour, and maintain a sense of proportion, you can take much of the hassle out of bargaining for your buys – colourful slippers, earthenware cooking utensils, carpets, clothing or striking jewellery. And, if it all gets too much, retire to a café for a soothing mint tea and watch the action from a distance.

A lane opposite the *Café de France* on the Djemaa el Fna leads to a stuccowork arch that marks the beginning of the crowded **Souk Smarine**, an important thoroughfare traditionally dominated by textiles. Just before the red ochre arch at its end, Souk Smarine narrows and you get a glimpse through the passageways to its right of the **Rahba Kedima**, a small and fairly ramshackle square whose most interesting features are its apothecary stalls and carpet sellers. At the end of Rahba Kedima, a passageway to the left gives access to another, smaller square – a bustling, carpet-draped area known as la **Criée Berbère**, which is where slave auctions used to be held.

Cutting back to **Souk el Kebir**, which by now has taken over from the Smarine, you emerge at the *kissarias*, the **covered markets** at the heart of the souk. *Kissarias* traditionally sell more expensive products, which today means a predominance of Western designs and imports. Off to their right is **Souk des Bijoutiers**, a modest jewellers' lane, while at the north end is a convoluted web of alleys comprising the **Souk Cherratin**, essentially a leatherworkers' market.

If you're keen to buy the best in the souk, you should study the more-or-less fixed prices of the range of crafts in the excellent **Ensemble Artesenal** (Mon–Sat 8.30am–1pm & 2.30–7pm, Sun 8.30am–noon), just inside the ramparts on Ave Mohammed V.

Flea markets in Paris

Shopping in Paris conjures images of chichi designer stores on Rue du Faubourg Saint-Honoré or funky fashion boutiques in the Marais. But there's another, older tradition that draws thousands of Parisians and eager tourists every weekend: the **flea market**, or *marché aux puces*. The markets originated two hundred years ago with makeshift stalls set up by the city's rag-and-bone men, who eventually migrated from the pickpocket-ridden centre to three sites outside the city walls. These three markets remain to this day, and amongst a fair amount of detritus you can find lithographs, fine furniture, antique toys, stamps, postcards, tapestries and much more.

Some traditions die hard – the markets are still beset by pickpockets, so be careful where you stash your cash. Serious shoppers should hit the markets in the early morning for the best bargains.

The markets

Les Puces de Saint-Ouen 48, rue Jules Vallès. Metro Porte de Clignacourt (line 4) or Porte de St-Ouen (line 13). Sat–Mon 7.30am–6pm. The biggest flea market in Paris features a wonderful jumble of collectibles: Art Deco mirrors, gilded furniture, Chinese antiquities and even whole staircases and marble tabletops. Good crèpe stands and cafés will keep you fuelled up.

Parisian flea market

Marché aux Puces de Montreuil Ave de la Porte de Montreuil; Metro Porte de Montreuil (line 9). Sat–Mon 7.30am–6pm. Not the place for fine antiques, but you will find some fun twentieth-century memorabilia.
Marché aux Puces de la Porte de Vanves Ave Georges Lafenestre & Ave Marc Sagnier. Metro Porte de Vanves (line 13). Sat & Sun: Ave Marc Sagnier till 1pm, Ave Georges Lafenestre till 6pm. This easily accessible market has trinkets, watches, photographs and all manner of other intriguing bits and pieces.

Interior design in Copenhagen

In a recent poll **Copenhagen** was voted the happiest capital in Europe, and the laid-back locals certainly seem pretty pleased as they cycle around their compact city. As well as enjoying the good life, Copenhagen also has an international reputation for the impeccable stylishness of its interior design. This derives squarely from Denmark's proudly egalitarian stance, the ethos being that good design should be affordable and available to all. Most influential of all Danish designers was Arne Jacobsen, whose iconic "Egg" and "Swan" chairs, created for the *Radisson SAS* hotel in Copenhagen in 1958, reflects a certain austerity in the Danish character as well as a reverence for natural forms. The *Radisson* in fact was the world's first designer hotel, with Jacobsen's vision informing every detail, and was an inspiration for designers the world over; original Jacobsen chairs, as well as Poul Henningsen lamps and Piet Hein tables, are still much prized in Denmark and beyond.

The official **Danish tourist board** website (®www.visitdenmark.com) has plenty more about Danish design, or check out ®www.visitcopenhagen.com for practical details about staying in the city. The Scandinavian airlines SAS and Sterling fly to Copenhagen from UK airports, as do Ryanair, easyJet and British Airways.

Take a break at Louisiana

No admirer of Danish style should miss the ten-kilometre train trip from Copenhagen to Humlebæk to visit **Louisiana** (Ⓦ www.louisiana.dk), an outstanding modern art gallery perched above the sea. Its setting alone is worth the journey, harmoniously combining art, architecture and the natural landscape, and visits to the galleries, garden and lovely café are guaranteed to soothe the senses. As well as a strong permanent collection including sculptures by Henry Moore and Giacometti, there's an intriguing programme of temporary exhibitions by Danish and international artists. The excellent shop sells funky perspex jewellery, art books and great games and gifts for kids.

Design stores and districts

Danish Design Centre Hans Christian Anderson Boulevard 27 Ⓦ www.ddc.dk. The shop here has a huge range of books in English on art and design, plus the fun "travel light" range of products for travel and adventure, and some smart gadgets that make great gifts.

Georg Jensen Amagertorv 4 Ⓦ www.georgjensen.com. Silverware specialists with a wonderful elegant range of bowls, candleholders, jugs and cutlery. Jacobsen strikes again with his 1957 minimalist cutlery, effortlessly modern and more cherished than ever.

Illums Bolighus Amagertorv 10 Ⓦ www.royalshopping.com. A design emporium with sleek furniture and some natty smaller pieces like the Hang It All coat-stand with its brightly coloured spheres that resembles a model of molecules, slim Gemini candleholders, and, for those who can't quite stretch to the real thing, miniature walnut Jacobsen chairs.

Nørrebro Trendy district that's good for secondhand design and furniture: shops are concentrated on Bredgade, with Danish design classics at Klassik (no. 3), Dansk Møbelkunst (no. 32), Permanent Design (no. 34) and Living Furniture (no. 45).

Paustian Kalkbrænderiløbskaj 2, Ⓦ www.paustian.dk. Located in a striking modernist building on the waterfront, its slender lines inspired by Danish beech forests. Stocks super-cool Danish and international home furnishings.

Fashion and antiques in Brussels

Brussels has long been a firm favourite for city breaks, boasting architecture and museums to rank with the best in Europe and a well-preserved medieval centre. The restaurants are of an excellent standard, and there's a plethora of elegant bars and sumptuous Art Nouveau cafés. But the city is also gaining a strong reputation for its shopping. As far as up-and-coming fashion goes, the place to be is Dansaert, with a plethora of intriguing and original **designers** showing their work, while you'll find the big names – Gucci, Armani, Chanel, Dior, Louis Vuitton, Hermès, Yves Saint Laurent, Tod's and Versace – in the swish Avenue Louise area. For **antique and vintage stores**, a good place to start exploring is the ancient Quartier Marolles. Place du Jeu de Balle, in the heart of the district, is the site of the city's best **flea market**, good for unearthing interesting costume jewellery

Belgian flea market

Antique Dealers' Fair

For discerning antique collectors, January's **Antique Dealers' Fair** (Ⓦ www.antiques-fair.be) is a date not to miss. It's held in the very heart of the city and boasts all manner of goodies – Old Master paintings, contemporary photography, medieval sculpture, porcelain and ceramics, books and manuscripts, Egyptian antiquities, a great variety of furniture and even pre-Columbian art. Reassuringly, everything on display is selected and authenticated by an independent panel, and there's a bilingual catalogue available.

– it's open daily from 7am, but is at its busiest on Sundays. More one-offs are provided at the Manufacture Belge de Dentelle (Ⓦ www.mbd.be), where you can pick out pieces of modern or antique lace.

There are plenty of flights here, but direct Eurostar trains from London get you to Brussels in under two hours – see Ⓦ www.belgiumtheplaceto.be for the lowdown on city practicalities.

Best boutiques

Azniv Afsar Rue Léon Lepage 30. One for the fashionistas: this is a funky boutique showcasing Afsar's beautiful geometric designs.

Chine Collection Ave Louise 82–84 Ⓦ www.chinecollection.com. Floaty, feminine and covetable, these Chinese-inspired garments are very flattering and easy to wear – they work well in layers.

Hatshoe Rue Antoine Dansaert 89. Brilliantly original footwear showcased in an Art Deco building; you can find shoes by Dries Van Noten amongst others.

Francis Ferent Ave Louise 60 Ⓦ www.ferent.be. A chichi boutique with a range of international designer offerings, from Stella McCartney to Dolce & Gabbana.

Stijl Rue Antoine Dansaert 74. Belgian design is promoted at Stijl, including Olivier Theyskens' spectacular garb, as worn by Madonna, and Ann Demeulemeester's elegant masculine chic.

Olivier Strelli Ave Louise 72 Ⓦ www.olivierstrelli.com. An established Belgian designer, his earthy palette inspired by the colours of the Belgian Congo where he grew up. Fabrics are soft, lines are fluid and all in all the clothes are wonderfully wearable.

Boutique, Brussels

Travel essentials

Entry requirements

Citizens of the UK need a valid **passport** but do not need a **visa** to enter most European countries. Major exceptions where visas are required (as far as this guide is concerned) are Turkey (visa available at port of entry) and Russia. For some countries, passports must be valid for at least six months beyond the end of the stay. If you're unsure, it's always worth checking with the embassy or consulate of the country you intend to visit (or ask your travel agent), as visa requirements for some countries can and do change.

Getting there

Budget **airlines** have brought virtually every country in Europe within easy reach of the UK, and prices start at next to nothing – sometimes with only the taxes to pay. For the best fares, book online as far in advance as possible and travel midweek if you can. Predictably, London's five airports (Heathrow, Gatwick, Stansted, Luton and City) have the widest choice of destinations, though Manchester has flights to most parts of Europe, and there are also convenient services from a wide array of regional airports, including Birmingham, Bristol, Cardiff, Glasgow, Edinburgh, Leeds/Bradford, Liverpool, Newcastle and Teesside.

Carbon offset schemes

Schemes run by Ⓦ www.climatecare.org, Ⓦ www.carbonneutral.com and others provide "carbon calculators" for working out the global-warming contribution of a specific flight, and then let you contribute an appropriate amount of money to fund offsetting measures – often run in conjunction with sustainable development schemes. Rough Guides, together with Lonely Planet and other concerned partners in the travel industry, are supporting a **carbon offset scheme** run by climatecare.org. Please take the time to view our website (Ⓦ www.roughguides.com/climatechange) and see how you can help to make your trip climate neutral.

It's easy to book flights, accommodation and other services yourself with an **online booking** agent, though if you prefer to have someone else make the arrangements contact a specialist **city break** operator.

For European destinations close to the UK **train travel** is fast becoming the logical alternative to packed airports and soaring CO2 emissions, and it's surprisingly speedy. Direct Eurostar trains through the Channel Tunnel from St Pancras International in London run to Lille (1hr 20min), Brussels (1hr 50min) and Paris (2hr 15min), as well as to Disneyland Resort (all year), Avignon (summer) and the French Alps (winter). Tickets start at £59 return, and there are onward connections from Brussels and Paris to destinations across Europe. Even places as far from the UK as Berlin, Prague or Madrid can all be reached relatively quickly by train, provided you don't mind viewing a night on the train as part of your break.

Airlines

Aer Lingus ⓦ www.aerlingus.com. Destinations across Ireland.
Air Berlin ⓦ www.airberlin.com. To many destinations in Spain, Portugal, Germany, Switzerland and Austria.
Air France ⓦ www.airfrance.co.uk. French national airline.
Alitalia ⓦ www.alitalia.com. Italian national airline
Austrian Airlines ⓦ www.aua.com. Austrian national airline.
bmi ⓦ www.flybmi.com. Extensive European routes.
bmibaby ⓦ www.bmibaby.com. Low-cost airline with extensive European routes.
British Airways ⓦ www.britishairways.com. British national airline.
easyJet ⓦ www.easyJet.com. Low-cost airline with extensive European routes.
Flybe ⓦ www.flybe.com. Low-cost airline with extensive European routes.
Iberia ⓦ www.iberia.com. Spanish national airline.
Jet2.com ⓦ www.jet2.com. Budget airline with extensive European destinations.
KLM ⓦ www.klm.com. Dutch national airline.
Olympic ⓦ www.olympic-airways.com. Greek national airline.
Royal Air Maroc ⓦ www.royalairmaroc.com. Moroccan national airline.
Ryanair ⓦ www.ryanair.com. Budget airline with extensive European routes.
SAS ⓦ www.flysas.com. Routes across Scandinavia.
Sky Europe ⓦ www.skyeurope.com. Central European low-coat airline – to Poland, Czech Republic and Austria.

Swiss ⓦ www.swiss.com. Swiss national airline.
TAP ⓦ www.tap-airportugal.co.uk. Portuguese national airline.
VLM Airlines ⓦ www.flyvlm.com. To Belgium and Netherlands.

City break operators

Cities Direct ⓦ www.citiesdirect.co.uk. City-break specialist, by plane and train.
Cresta Holidays ⓦ www.crestaholidays.co.uk. European short-break specialists.
Eurobreak ⓦ www.eurobreak.co.uk. Cities and short breaks across Europe, including St Petersburg.
Thomson ⓦ www.thomsoncities.co.uk. Major tour operator with city-break arm.

Online bookings

ⓦ **www.ebookers.com** Low fares on an extensive selection of scheduled airfares and package deals.
ⓦ **www.expedia.co.uk** Search and book flights, hotels and rental cars.
ⓦ **www.flights4less.co.uk** Good for discounted airfares.
ⓦ **www.lastminute.com** Book flights, city breaks, hotels, car hire, theatre tickets and more.

Train contacts

Eurostar ⓦ www.eurostar.com. Direct train bookings across France, Belgium and the Netherlands, plus city break and hotel deals.
Ffestiniog Travel ⓦ www.festtravel.co.uk. Rail tour operator with plenty of experience - also a good stop for booking railway tickets anywhere in Europe.
Great Railway Journeys ⓦ www.greatrail.com. For "journeys as great as the destinations", from Morocco to Scandinavia.
Man in Seat 61 ⓦ www.seat61.com. Idiosyncratic? Most definitely, but has incredibly detailed advice about rail travel from Britain to any European country.
Rail Europe ⓦ www.raileurope.co.uk. The UK's leading supplier of European rail tickets and passes.
Trainseurope ⓦ www.trainseurope.co.uk. Train tickets for short hops and long-distance travel, plus European rail passes.

All aboard!

Kick off your train journey from St Pancras International, and you can have a glass of bubbly at Europe's longest champagne bar, before embarking on your journey. Or consider one of the following **classic train routes**, which can all be booked through a specialist rail tour operator.

Al Andalus ⓦ www.spanish-rail.co.uk.
A stylish Belle Epoque train, which takes you from Seville to Cordoba and Ronda in the height of luxury.

Glacier Express ⓦ www.glacierexpress.ch. A panoramic trip through the Swiss Alps – 291 bridges, 91 tunnels and 2000m altitude.

Orient Express ⓦ www.orient-express.com. Variations on the wonderfully romantic Paris–Venice route take you to Krakow, Warsaw and Prague.

Royal Scotsman ⓦ www.royalscotsman.com. Sweep through the mighty Scottish Highlands in an exclusive mahogany-lined carriage.

El Trancantabrico ⓦ www.transcantabrico.feve.es. Indulge in an on-board hydro-sauna as you traverse northern Spain.

Insurance and health

All EU citizens resident in the UK and Ireland are covered by reciprocal health agreements for most of the countries covered in this book (the main exceptions are Morocco, Turkey and Romania). In practice, to claim local health treatment while on holiday you will often only need your passport, but it's safest to carry a **European Health Insurance card** (see ⓦ www.ehic.org.uk for full details), which will entitle you to treatment under the same conditions as local residents.

Even on the shortest of trips it's essential to take out **travel insurance**, just in case things go wrong. Rough Guides has teamed up with Columbus Direct to offer you travel insurance that can be tailored to suit your needs, from a short-break option for city getaways to annual multi-trip policies. Go to our website – ⓦ www.roughguidesinsurance.com – where you can purchase the insurance, or call ⓣ 0800/083 9507.

Keeping in touch

If you're taking your **mobile phone** with you, check with your service provider about coverage in the country to which you're travelling, and what the charges for use are likely to be. You may also have to get a different access code if you want to retrieve messages from your voicemail while you're abroad. You'll have no problem finding **internet access** wherever you go – though obviously it's easiest in the biggest cities. Most of the larger hotels in Europe have business centres with internet access, but this is almost always far more expensive than simply going down the street to the nearest internet café. Finally, British daily **newspapers** are widely available across Europe, often on the day of publication (in special European editions) or a day later.

Maps

Rough Guide maps are printed on rip-proof, waterproof paper – an ideal companion on a European mini break. There are country and regional maps available, covering the Algarve to Tuscany, Czech Republic to Turkey; and also city maps, from Amsterdam to Prague. You can buy or order them from any good bookshop, or buy online at ®www.roughguides.com.

Money, banks and exchange

Hotels, shops and restaurants across Europe accept major **credit and debit cards**, although you can't take this for granted, so always be sure to have some cash to hand. More importantly, you can use the cards 24/7 to get cash out of **ATMs** throughout Europe, including Morocco and Turkey, as long as they are affiliated to an international network (such as Visa, Mastercard or Cirrus). Note that cash withdrawals and credit card transactions are often subject to a fee, while both credit and debit cards may also impose a limit on the amount you can draw at one time, or in one day. If you're not sure whether your card will work, check with the issuer before you leave home.

Discounts and ID cards

It's worth taking any professional or age-related ID cards you may have, since many galleries, museums, tour operators and transport companies across Europe offer discounts to teachers, students, members of the armed forces, and senior citizens.

Traveller's cheques, in either euros or UK pounds, are a useful back-up source of funds but they're expensive: you'll usually have to pay commission when you buy the cheques and again when you cash them. The most commonly accepted brands are Thomas Cook/Mastercard, American Express and Visa. Most companies claim to replace lost or stolen cheques within 24 hours.

For **changing money abroad**, banks usually offer the best exchange rates. Outside normal hours you can often resort to **bureaux de change**, though their rates and/or commissions may well be less favourable. Automatic money-changing machines can also be handy out of hours, but don't give good exchange rates. Avoid changing money or cheques in hotels, where the exchange rates are generally very poor.

Recommended reading

You've probably already packed your holiday reading, but why not look out for one of these classics of European travel and adventure?

A Year in Provence Peter Mayle. Man moves to France in search of a new life in the sun – and has a lot to answer for.

A Time of Gifts Patrick Leigh Fermor. On foot from the Hook of Holland to Constantinople, in the company of a lyrical, gifted writer.

Driving Over Lemons Chris Stewart. Self-confessed "optimist in Andalucia" lives the good life in the foothills of Spain's Sierra Nevada.

Neither Here Nor There Bill Bryson. Witty American retraces his student travels in Europe, and can't decide whether it was awesome or awful.

The Art of Travel Alain de Botton. The philosophy of travel – how we prefigure places in our minds before we set off, and how we retain the memory of beautiful sights.

Trieste and the Meaning of Nowhere Jan Morris. The historian and lifelong traveller describes both Trieste and herself as being "on a fold in the map".

Safety

Travelling around Europe should be relatively trouble-free. However, conditions do vary greatly from, say, Scandinavia, where you're unlikely to encounter many problems, to poorer regions like Morocco and Turkey, where tourists tend to stand out more. Best advice: don't do anything, or go anywhere, that you wouldn't feel comfortable with at home. Keep valuables out of view and your bag always in view; leave your passport at the hotel; use sense when moving about late at night, and take a taxi back if in doubt. If you do have anything stolen you always need to **inform the local police** to get a statement for your insurance company.

Tourist information

Most European countries have a **national tourism office** while city and regional tourist offices in each country will be able to help you with accommodation, transport and other enquiries. We've provided useful websites throughout this guide, official or otherwise – and don't forget to go to ⓦ**www.roughguides.com** for plenty more advice and ideas about travelling in Europe.

Tourist information websites

Austria ⓦwww.austria.info.
Belgium ⓦwww.visitbelgium.com.
Czech Republic ⓦwww.czechtourism.com.
Denmark ⓦwww.visitdenmark.com.
England ⓦwww.enjoyengland.com.
France ⓦwww.franceguide.com.
Germany ⓦwww.germany-tourism.de.
Ireland ⓦwww.ireland.ie.
Italy ⓦwww.enit.it.
Netherlands ⓦwww.holland.com.
Poland ⓦwww.polandtour.org.
Portugal ⓦwww.visitportugal.com.
Romania ⓦwww.romaniatourism.com.
Scotland ⓦwww.visitscotland.com.
Spain ⓦwww.spain.info.
Sweden ⓦwww.visitsweden.com.
Switzerland ⓦwww.myswitzerland.com.
Wales ⓦwww.visitwales.co.uk.

Index

G

H

I

K

L

M

N

O

P

R

S

Picture credits

All images copyright Rough Guides except the following:

Front cover image: Bicycle and tulips, Amsterdam © Marc Romanelli/Alamy

Back cover image: Man with gondola, Venice © Diana Jarvis

Black and white images:

p.3 &125 Woman looking out of a train window © Walter Smith/Corbis

p.4 Woman with paper and coffee © Ghislain & Marie David de Lossy/Getty Images

p.8 The Eiffel Tower and cherry blossom © Michael Mcqueen/Getty Images

p.13 & 14 Guggenheim ©The Steve Bicknell Style Library/Alamy

p.21 Visitor admiring the temple of the Parthenon © John Kolesidis/Corbis

p.29 & 30 Lisbon Tram © Hans Georg Roth/Corbis

p.43 Gamia Stan Café and Storkyrkan, Stockholm © Jon Hicks/Corbis

p.47 & 48 Woman browsing books © Homer Sykes/Alamy

p.55 Couples waltzing at Vienna Opera © Reuter Raymond/Corbis

p.87 & 88 Horse Drawn Sleigh © Rob Howard/Corbis

p.99&100 Woman practicing Yoga by Lake © Michael A.Keller/Corbis

p.103 Woman enjoying facial © Adam Woolfitt/Corbis

p.109 Canopy Bed with Sheer Curtain © Remi Benali/Corbis

p.121 Woman at jewellery stall © Corbis